# THE COLORADO RECREATIONAL CANNABIS USER'S HANDBOOK

## By Michael Malott

**Forward by Dennis Peron**

*Although at this time the State of Colorado currently allows the recreational and medical use of marijuana under state law.*
*Federal Law supersedes state law.*
*Under Federal Law, marijuana is designated as a schedule 1 drug and is illegal by Federal Law under any and all circumstances.*

This book could be dedicated to
Two of my cannabis heroes
## JACK HERER & PAUL CORNWELL

## Acknowledgments

Sincere thanks to Paul Cornwell, Mason Tvert, Dennis Peron and Ed Rosenthal. Also thanks to Dale Gieringer, Ph.D., Jack Herer, Steve DeAngelo, Jeff Jones, Willie Nelson for your continued support, Dale Sky Jones and the folks at Oaksterdam, D.J. Short, Dr. Lester Grinspoon, Brian Peron, Tommy, Paris & Shelby Chong, Steve Kelnhofer & Connie at 7th Floor Llc., & the Silver Surfer crew, Claudia@Sensi Seeds, Rollie and the folks at Pure Hemp Papers. Thanks to CAMP, Coalition for Abolition of Marijuana Prohibition and least and last Jeff Davis, thanks for letting me down!!

**Contact the author:**
**marijuanahandbook@hotmail.com**

**Author's Agent:**
**Cannabis Action Agency**
**CAATalent@hotmail.com**

# TABLE OF CONTENTS

# FOREWORD

By
Dennis Peron
The Father of Medical Marijuana

I didn't invent medical marijuana. I brought the wisdom of the ancients to the modern world. The ancient Chinese Pharmacopoeia, for example, lists marijuana in treatment for such afflictions as menstrual cramps, rheumatism, and arthritis. Medicines that were suited for humans in those days are just as suited today.

In 1988 during the AIDS epidemic of San Francisco, my lover Jonathan West was stricken with the disease. These were the days before protease inhibitors. We had no medicines. Smoking and eating marijuana helped Jonathan retain his appetite when he contracted a form of related cancer, helped relieve his neuropathy (tingling in his extremities), and alleviated his nausea from chemotherapy. It was a miracle drug, and it was available.

Unfortunately, marijuana did not cure him. But it alleviated his pain and greatly helped him feel better, to cope with the terrible symptoms of his illness. When Jonathan died in 1990, I made a commitment to him to help other people like himself, to make marijuana available to those who suffer from this terrible disease from which there was no cure.

My first act was to sponsor an initiative on the 1991 San Francisco ballot to not prosecute people using marijuana for medicinal purposes. It won by 80% vote. It was my first eulogy to Jonathan. This encouraged me to go to the California State Legislature to enact three bills in 1992, '93 and '95 to protect marijuana patients.

All three passed with bi-partisan support. All three were vetoed by then Governor Pete Wilson (R).

Refusing to give up the fight, I worked to combine language from all three bills into a single initiative titled the Compassionate Use Act of 1996, also known as Proposition 215. Against all odds, I collected one million signatures.

By this time I had been running the San Francisco Cannabis Buyer's Club for 6 years without getting busted. I had convinced the Mayor and the Chief of Police to not interfere with our operations in the name of compassion for those suffering with AIDS – which by this time was 40,000 people in San Francisco. The Club had grown to 15,000 members. It had begun with AIDS patients – then drawn cancer patients, MS patients, those with glaucoma. The toughest call for me was admitting those who claimed they were depressed: but many doctors began recommending depressed patients, several of whom were suicidal. It was through my experiences at the club that I was taught the real value of medical marijuana, how it could be safely used to treat the symptoms of a broad range of illnesses.

Keeping that in mind, when I wrote Proposition 215 I wanted marijuana to be available for everyone who found that it helped alleviate their suffering from symptoms of any malady. It would protect doctors who prescribed it from prosecution or denial of rights to practice, and allow patients, with doctor's recommendation, to obtain, possess and cultivate marijuana for medical purposes without fear of being a criminal.

My own illness is alcoholism. Since becoming a marijuana user with my doctor's recommendation, I have not had a drink in 31 years. Without marijuana, I would be a lush.

Again, against all odds– Proposition 215 passed with by 56%, a million more votes than Bill Clinton who took the state.

We received endorsements from doctors, nurses, religious leaders, teachers, cancer patients --- a full spectrum of America.

My greatest opposition was from the narcs. They came from the California Narcotics Association – acting like pigs at the trough -- led by my nemesis, Dan Lungren, Attorney General of California. Lungren took the initiative to close the Cannabis Buyer's Club with a show of force – hundreds of fully armed narcotics agents marching in and closing down the Club which occupied a four story building on Market Street. I dubbed it the "Four Story Felony."

It was in October, just before the election, that they arrested me for selling marijuana in a neighboring county, Alameda, hoping to paint the Cannabis Buyer's Club as a reason not to vote for Prop 215.

In reality the exposure gave us a 2 % boost in the polls: thank you, Dan Lundgren!

The charges against me were thrown out.

The successful passing of Prop 215 in California was a shot heard around the world. It spawned movements to legalize medical marijuana use around the country and circled the globe. From that vote, thousands of cannabis buyers clubs sprung up to serve the sick in a quasi-legal form.

At a press conference after the 1996 election, I stated:

All Marijuana use has a medical component.

People use it because it makes them feel better, which is a medical reason.

To date, 15 states have passed laws to legalize the use of medical marijuana and ten states are pending.

Colorado's passing of legal medical marijuana legislature contributes a substantial portion of the US electoral vote to continue to demand the rescheduling of marijuana to become a legally prescribed medicine in this country.

This issue is about freedom, more than it's about marijuana: Freedom for patients and freedom for doctors from government intrusion on our lives; freedom of choice of treatment for and from the pain and suffering of the debilitating symptoms of disease.

I salute my good friend, Michael Malott for publishing this handbook for explaining the uses of medical marijuana by enlightening all of us in a simple, straightforward manner. It should be in the hands of every person who gains benefit from the use of medical marijuana.

It's been a long, difficult battle. In the end, the good guys are winning. We are changing the world for the better in the name of love, loss, and compassion.

In the loving memory of my partner, Jonathan West, this is my gift from the ancients to the people of today and to the future.


----Dennis Peron
San Francisco, California

13

# Amendment 64: The Regulate Marijuana Like Alcohol Act of 2012

Be it Enacted by the People of the State of Colorado

Article XVIII of the constitution of the state of Colorado is amended BY THE ADDITION OF A NEW SECTION to read:

**Section 16. Personal use and regulation of marijuana**

**(1) Purpose and findings.**

    (a) IN THE INTEREST OF THE EFFICIENT USE OF LAW ENFORCEMENT RESOURCES, ENHANCING REVENUE FOR PUBLIC PURPOSES, AND INDIVIDUAL FREEDOM, THE PEOPLE OF THE STATE OF COLORADO FIND AND DECLARE THAT THE USE OF MARIJUANA SHOULD BE LEGAL FOR PERSONS TWENTY-ONE YEARS OF AGE OR OLDER AND TAXED IN A MANNER SIMILAR TO ALCOHOL.

    (b) IN THE INTEREST OF THE HEALTH AND PUBLIC SAFETY OF OUR CITIZENRY, THE PEOPLE OF THE STATE OF COLORADO FURTHER FIND AND DECLARE THAT MARIJUANA SHOULD BE REGULATED IN A MANNER SIMILAR TO ALCOHOL SO THAT:

    (I) INDIVIDUALS WILL HAVE TO SHOW PROOF OF AGE BEFORE PURCHASING MARIJUANA;

    (II) SELLING, DISTRIBUTING, OR TRANSFERRING MARIJUANA TO MINORS AND OTHER INDIVIDUALS UNDER THE AGE OF TWENTY-ONE SHALL REMAIN ILLEGAL;

    (III) DRIVING UNDER THE INFLUENCE OF MARIJUANA SHALL REMAIN ILLEGAL;

    (IV) LEGITIMATE, TAXPAYING BUSINESS

PEOPLE, AND NOT CRIMINAL ACTORS, WILL CONDUCT SALES OF MARIJUANA; AND

(V) MARIJUANA SOLD IN THIS STATE WILL BE LABELED AND SUBJECT TO ADDITIONAL REGULATIONS TO ENSURE THAT CONSUMERS ARE INFORMED AND PROTECTED.

(c) IN THE INTEREST OF ENACTING RATIONAL POLICIES FOR THE TREATMENT OF ALL VARIATIONS OF THE CANNABIS PLANT, THE PEOPLE OF COLORADO FURTHER FIND AND DECLARE THAT INDUSTRIAL HEMP SHOULD BE REGULATED SEPARATELY FROM STRAINS OF CANNABIS WITH HIGHER DELTA-9 TETRAHYDROCANNABINOL (THC) CONCENTRATIONS.

(d) THE PEOPLE OF THE STATE OF COLORADO FURTHER FIND AND DECLARE THAT IT IS NECESSARY TO ENSURE CONSISTENCY AND FAIRNESS IN THE APPLICATION OF THIS SECTION THROUGHOUT THE STATE AND THAT, THEREFORE, THE MATTERS ADDRESSED BY THIS SECTION ARE, EXCEPT AS SPECIFIED HEREIN, MATTERS OF STATEWIDE CONCERN.

**(2) Definitions.** AS USED IN THIS SECTION, UNLESS THE CONTEXT OTHERWISE REQUIRES,

(a) "COLORADO MEDICAL MARIJUANA CODE" MEANS ARTICLE 43.3 OF TITLE 12, COLORADO REVISED STATUTES.

(b) "CONSUMER" MEANS A PERSON TWENTY-ONE YEARS OF AGE OR OLDER WHO PURCHASES MARIJUANA OR MARIJUANA PRODUCTS FOR PERSONAL USE BY PERSONS TWENTY-ONE YEARS OF AGE OR OLDER, BUT NOT FOR RESALE TO OTHERS.

(c) "DEPARTMENT" MEANS THE DEPARTMENT OF REVENUE OR ITS SUCCESSOR AGENCY.

(d) "INDUSTRIAL HEMP" MEANS THE PLANT OF THE GENUS CANNABIS AND ANY PART OF SUCH PLANT, WHETHER GROWING OR NOT, WITH A DELTA-9 TETRAHYDROCANNABINOL CONCENTRATION THAT DOES NOT EXCEED THREE-TENTHS PERCENT ON A DRY WEIGHT BASIS.

(e) "LOCALITY" MEANS A COUNTY, MUNICIPALITY, OR CITY AND COUNTY.

(f) "MARIJUANA" OR "MARIHUANA" MEANS ALL PARTS OF THE PLANT OF THE GENUS CANNABIS WHETHER GROWING OR NOT, THE SEEDS THEREOF, THE RESIN EXTRACTED FROM ANY PART OF THE PLANT, AND EVERY COMPOUND, MANUFACTURE, SALT, DERIVATIVE, MIXTURE, OR PREPARATION OF THE PLANT, ITS SEEDS, OR ITS RESIN, INCLUDING MARIHUANA CONCENTRATE. "MARIJUANA" OR "MARIHUANA" DOES NOT INCLUDE INDUSTRIAL HEMP, NOR DOES IT INCLUDE FIBER PRODUCED FROM THE STALKS, OIL, OR CAKE MADE FROM THE SEEDS OF THE PLANT, STERILIZED SEED OF THE PLANT WHICH IS INCAPABLE OF GERMINATION, OR THE WEIGHT OF ANY OTHER INGREDIENT COMBINED WITH MARIJUANA TO PREPARE TOPICAL OR ORAL ADMINISTRATIONS, FOOD, DRINK, OR OTHER PRODUCT.

(g) "MARIJUANA ACCESSORIES" MEANS ANY EQUIPMENT, PRODUCTS, OR MATERIALS OF ANY KIND WHICH ARE USED, INTENDED FOR USE, OR DESIGNED FOR USE IN PLANTING, PROPAGATING, CULTIVATING, GROWING, HARVESTING, COMPOSTING, MANUFACTURING, COMPOUNDING, CONVERTING, PRODUCING, PROCESSING, PREPARING, TESTING, ANALYZING, PACKAGING, REPACKAGING, STORING, VAPORIZING, OR CONTAINING MARIJUANA, OR FOR INGESTING, INHALING, OR OTHERWISE INTRODUCING

MARIJUANA INTO THE HUMAN BODY.

(h) "MARIJUANA CULTIVATION FACILITY" MEANS AN ENTITY LICENSED TO CULTIVATE, PREPARE, AND PACKAGE MARIJUANA AND SELL MARIJUANA TO RETAIL MARIJUANA STORES, TO MARIJUANA PRODUCT MANUFACTURING FACILITIES, AND TO OTHER MARIJUANA CULTIVATION FACILITIES, BUT NOT TO CONSUMERS.

(i) "MARIJUANA ESTABLISHMENT" MEANS A MARIJUANA CULTIVATION FACILITY, A MARIJUANA TESTING FACILITY, A MARIJUANA PRODUCT MANUFACTURING FACILITY, OR A RETAIL MARIJUANA STORE.

(j) "MARIJUANA PRODUCT MANUFACTURING FACILITY" MEANS AN ENTITY LICENSED TO PURCHASE MARIJUANA; MANUFACTURE, PREPARE, AND PACKAGE MARIJUANA PRODUCTS; AND SELL MARIJUANA AND MARIJUANA PRODUCTS TO OTHER MARIJUANA PRODUCT MANUFACTURING FACILITIES AND TO RETAIL MARIJUANA STORES, BUT NOT TO CONSUMERS.

(k) "MARIJUANA PRODUCTS" MEANS CONCENTRATED MARIJUANA PRODUCTS AND MARIJUANA PRODUCTS THAT ARE COMPRISED OF MARIJUANA AND OTHER INGREDIENTS AND ARE INTENDED FOR USE OR CONSUMPTION, SUCH AS, BUT NOT LIMITED TO, EDIBLE PRODUCTS, OINTMENTS, AND TINCTURES.

(l) "MARIJUANA TESTING FACILITY" MEANS AN ENTITY LICENSED TO ANALYZE AND CERTIFY THE SAFETY AND POTENCY OF MARIJUANA.

(m) "MEDICAL MARIJUANA CENTER" MEANS AN ENTITY LICENSED BY A STATE AGENCY TO SELL MARIJUANA AND MARIJUANA PRODUCTS PURSUANT TO SECTION 14 OF THIS ARTICLE AND

THE COLORADO MEDICAL MARIJUANA CODE.
(n) "RETAIL MARIJUANA STORE" MEANS AN ENTITY LICENSED TO PURCHASE MARIJUANA FROM MARIJUANA CULTIVATION FACILITIES AND MARIJUANA AND MARIJUANA PRODUCTS FROM MARIJUANA PRODUCT MANUFACTURING FACILITIES AND TO SELL MARIJUANA AND MARIJUANA PRODUCTS TO CONSUMERS.
(o) "UNREASONABLY IMPRACTICABLE" MEANS THAT THE MEASURES NECESSARY TO COMPLY WITH THE REGULATIONS REQUIRE SUCH A HIGH INVESTMENT OF RISK, MONEY, TIME, OR ANY OTHER RESOURCE OR ASSET THAT THE OPERATION OF A MARIJUANA ESTABLISHMENT IS NOT WORTHY OF BEING CARRIED OUT IN PRACTICE BY A REASONABLY PRUDENT BUSINESSPERSON.

**(3) Personal use of marijuana.** NOTWITHSTANDING ANY OTHER PROVISION OF LAW, THE FOLLOWING ACTS ARE NOT UNLAWFUL AND SHALL NOT BE AN OFFENSE UNDER COLORADO LAW OR THE LAW OF ANY LOCALITY WITHIN COLORADO OR BE A BASIS FOR SEIZURE OR FORFEITURE OF ASSETS UNDER COLORADO LAW FOR PERSONS TWENTY-ONE YEARS OF AGE OR OLDER:
(a) POSSESSING, USING, DISPLAYING, PURCHASING, OR TRANSPORTING MARIJUANA ACCESSORIES OR ONE OUNCE OR LESS OF MARIJUANA.
(b) POSSESSING, GROWING, PROCESSING, OR TRANSPORTING NO MORE THAN SIX MARIJUANA PLANTS, WITH THREE OR FEWER BEING MATURE, FLOWERING PLANTS, AND POSSESSION OF THE MARIJUANA PRODUCED BY THE PLANTS ON THE PREMISES WHERE THE PLANTS WERE GROWN, PROVIDED THAT THE GROWING TAKES PLACE IN AN ENCLOSED, LOCKED SPACE, IS NOT CONDUCTED

OPENLY OR PUBLICLY, AND IS NOT MADE AVAILABLE FOR SALE.
(c) TRANSFER OF ONE OUNCE OR LESS OF MARIJUANA WITHOUT REMUNERATION TO A PERSON WHO IS TWENTY-ONE YEARS OF AGE OR OLDER.
(d) CONSUMPTION OF MARIJUANA, PROVIDED THAT NOTHING IN THIS SECTION SHALL PERMIT CONSUMPTION THAT IS CONDUCTED OPENLY AND PUBLICLY OR IN A MANNER THAT ENDANGERS OTHERS.
(e) ASSISTING ANOTHER PERSON WHO IS TWENTY-ONE YEARS OF AGE OR OLDER IN ANY OF THE ACTS DESCRIBED IN PARAGRAPHS (a) THROUGH (d) OF THIS SUBSECTION.

**(4) Lawful operation of marijuana-related facilities.** NOTWITHSTANDING ANY OTHER PROVISION OF LAW, THE FOLLOWING ACTS ARE NOT UNLAWFUL AND SHALL NOT BE AN OFFENSE UNDER COLORADO LAW OR BE A BASIS FOR SEIZURE OR FORFEITURE OF ASSETS UNDER COLORADO LAW FOR PERSONS TWENTY-ONE YEARS OF AGE OR OLDER:
(a) MANUFACTURE, POSSESSION, OR PURCHASE OF MARIJUANA ACCESSORIES OR THE SALE OF MARIJUANA ACCESSORIES TO A PERSON WHO IS TWENTY-ONE YEARS OF AGE OR OLDER.
(b) POSSESSING, DISPLAYING, OR TRANSPORTING MARIJUANA OR MARIJUANA PRODUCTS; PURCHASE OF MARIJUANA FROM A MARIJUANA CULTIVATION FACILITY; PURCHASE OF MARIJUANA OR MARIJUANA PRODUCTS FROM A MARIJUANA PRODUCT MANUFACTURING FACILITY; OR SALE OF MARIJUANA OR MARIJUANA PRODUCTS TO CONSUMERS, IF THE PERSON CONDUCTING THE ACTIVITIES DESCRIBED IN THIS PARAGRAPH HAS

OBTAINED A CURRENT, VALID LICENSE TO OPERATE A RETAIL MARIJUANA STORE OR IS ACTING IN HIS OR HER CAPACITY AS AN OWNER, EMPLOYEE OR AGENT OF A LICENSED RETAIL MARIJUANA STORE.

(c) CULTIVATING, HARVESTING, PROCESSING, PACKAGING, TRANSPORTING, DISPLAYING, OR POSSESSING MARIJUANA; DELIVERY OR TRANSFER OF MARIJUANA TO A MARIJUANA TESTING FACILITY; SELLING MARIJUANA TO A MARIJUANA CULTIVATION FACILITY, A MARIJUANA PRODUCT MANUFACTURING FACILITY, OR A RETAIL MARIJUANA STORE; OR THE PURCHASE OF MARIJUANA FROM A MARIJUANA CULTIVATION FACILITY, IF THE PERSON CONDUCTING THE ACTIVITIES DESCRIBED IN THIS PARAGRAPH HAS OBTAINED A CURRENT, VALID LICENSE TO OPERATE A MARIJUANA CULTIVATION FACILITY OR IS ACTING IN HIS OR HER CAPACITY AS AN OWNER, EMPLOYEE, OR AGENT OF A LICENSED MARIJUANA CULTIVATION FACILITY.

(d) PACKAGING, PROCESSING, TRANSPORTING, MANUFACTURING, DISPLAYING, OR POSSESSING MARIJUANA OR MARIJUANA PRODUCTS; DELIVERY OR TRANSFER OF MARIJUANA OR MARIJUANA PRODUCTS TO A MARIJUANA TESTING FACILITY; SELLING MARIJUANA OR MARIJUANA PRODUCTS TO A RETAIL MARIJUANA STORE OR A MARIJUANA PRODUCT MANUFACTURING FACILITY; THE PURCHASE OF MARIJUANA FROM A MARIJUANA CULTIVATION FACILITY; OR THE PURCHASE OF MARIJUANA OR MARIJUANA PRODUCTS FROM A MARIJUANA PRODUCT MANUFACTURING FACILITY, IF THE PERSON CONDUCTING THE ACTIVITIES

DESCRIBED IN THIS PARAGRAPH HAS OBTAINED A CURRENT, VALID LICENSE TO OPERATE A MARIJUANA PRODUCT MANUFACTURING FACILITY OR IS ACTING IN HIS OR HER CAPACITY AS AN OWNER, EMPLOYEE, OR AGENT OF A LICENSED MARIJUANA PRODUCT MANUFACTURING FACILITY.

(e) POSSESSING, CULTIVATING, PROCESSING, REPACKAGING, STORING, TRANSPORTING, DISPLAYING, TRANSFERRING OR DELIVERING MARIJUANA OR MARIJUANA PRODUCTS IF THE PERSON HAS OBTAINED A CURRENT, VALID LICENSE TO OPERATE A MARIJUANA TESTING FACILITY OR IS ACTING IN HIS OR HER CAPACITY AS AN OWNER, EMPLOYEE, OR AGENT OF A LICENSED MARIJUANA TESTING FACILITY.

(f) LEASING OR OTHERWISE ALLOWING THE USE OF PROPERTY OWNED, OCCUPIED OR CONTROLLED BY ANY PERSON, CORPORATION OR OTHER ENTITY FOR ANY OF THE ACTIVITIES CONDUCTED LAWFULLY IN ACCORDANCE WITH PARAGRAPHS (a) THROUGH (e) OF THIS SUBSECTION.

**(5) Regulation of marijuana.**

(a) NOT LATER THAN JULY 1, 2013, THE DEPARTMENT SHALL ADOPT REGULATIONS NECESSARY FOR IMPLEMENTATION OF THIS SECTION. SUCH REGULATIONS SHALL NOT PROHIBIT THE OPERATION OF MARIJUANA ESTABLISHMENTS, EITHER EXPRESSLY OR THROUGH REGULATIONS THAT MAKE THEIR OPERATION UNREASONABLY IMPRACTICABLE. SUCH REGULATIONS SHALL INCLUDE:

(I) PROCEDURES FOR THE ISSUANCE, RENEWAL, SUSPENSION, AND REVOCATION OF A LICENSE TO OPERATE A MARIJUANA ESTABLISHMENT, WITH SUCH PROCEDURES

SUBJECT TO ALL REQUIREMENTS OF ARTICLE 4 OF TITLE 24 OF THE COLORADO ADMINISTRATIVE PROCEDURE ACT OR ANY SUCCESSOR PROVISION;

(II) A SCHEDULE OF APPLICATION, LICENSING AND RENEWAL FEES, PROVIDED, APPLICATION FEES SHALL NOT EXCEED FIVE THOUSAND DOLLARS, WITH THIS UPPER LIMIT ADJUSTED ANNUALLY FOR INFLATION, UNLESS THE DEPARTMENT DETERMINES A GREATER FEE IS NECESSARY TO CARRY OUT ITS RESPONSIBILITIES UNDER THIS SECTION, AND PROVIDED FURTHER, AN ENTITY THAT IS LICENSED UNDER THE COLORADO MEDICAL MARIJUANA CODE TO CULTIVATE OR SELL MARIJUANA OR TO MANUFACTURE MARIJUANA PRODUCTS AT THE TIME THIS SECTION TAKES EFFECT AND THAT CHOOSES TO APPLY FOR A SEPARATE MARIJUANA ESTABLISHMENT LICENSE SHALL NOT BE REQUIRED TO PAY AN APPLICATION FEE GREATER THAN FIVE HUNDRED DOLLARS TO APPLY FOR A LICENSE TO OPERATE A MARIJUANA ESTABLISHMENT IN ACCORDANCE WITH THE PROVISIONS OF THIS SECTION;

(III) QUALIFICATIONS FOR LICENSURE THAT ARE DIRECTLY AND DEMONSTRABLY RELATED TO THE OPERATION OF A MARIJUANA ESTABLISHMENT;

(IV) SECURITY REQUIREMENTS FOR MARIJUANA ESTABLISHMENTS;

(V) REQUIREMENTS TO PREVENT THE SALE OR DIVERSION OF MARIJUANA AND MARIJUANA PRODUCTS TO PERSONS UNDER THE AGE OF TWENTY-ONE;

(VI) LABELING REQUIREMENTS FOR MARIJUANA AND MARIJUANA PRODUCTS SOLD OR DISTRIBUTED BY A MARIJUANA ESTABLISHMENT;

(VII) HEALTH AND SAFETY REGULATIONS

AND STANDARDS FOR THE MANUFACTURE OF MARIJUANA PRODUCTS AND THE CULTIVATION OF MARIJUANA;

(VIII) RESTRICTIONS ON THE ADVERTISING AND DISPLAY OF MARIJUANA AND MARIJUANA PRODUCTS; AND

(IX) CIVIL PENALTIES FOR THE FAILURE TO COMPLY WITH REGULATIONS MADE PURSUANT TO THIS SECTION.

(b) IN ORDER TO ENSURE THE MOST SECURE, RELIABLE, AND ACCOUNTABLE SYSTEM FOR THE PRODUCTION AND DISTRIBUTION OF MARIJUANA AND MARIJUANA PRODUCTS IN ACCORDANCE WITH THIS SUBSECTION, IN ANY COMPETITIVE APPLICATION PROCESS THE DEPARTMENT SHALL HAVE AS A PRIMARY CONSIDERATION WHETHER AN APPLICANT:

(I) HAS PRIOR EXPERIENCE PRODUCING OR DISTRIBUTING MARIJUANA OR MARIJUANA PRODUCTS PURSUANT TO SECTION 14 OF THIS ARTICLE AND THE COLORADO MEDICAL MARIJUANA CODE IN THE LOCALITY IN WHICH THE APPLICANT SEEKS TO OPERATE A MARIJUANA ESTABLISHMENT; AND

(II) HAS, DURING THE EXPERIENCE DESCRIBED IN SUBPARAGRAPH (I), COMPLIED CONSISTENTLY WITH SECTION 14 OF THIS ARTICLE, THE PROVISIONS OF THE COLORADO MEDICAL MARIJUANA CODE AND CONFORMING REGULATIONS.

(c) IN ORDER TO ENSURE THAT INDIVIDUAL PRIVACY IS PROTECTED, NOTWITHSTANDING PARAGRAPH (a), THE DEPARTMENT SHALL NOT REQUIRE A CONSUMER TO PROVIDE A RETAIL MARIJUANA STORE WITH PERSONAL INFORMATION OTHER THAN GOVERNMENT-ISSUED

IDENTIFICATION TO DETERMINE THE CONSUMER'S AGE, AND A RETAIL MARIJUANA STORE SHALL NOT BE REQUIRED TO ACQUIRE AND RECORD PERSONAL INFORMATION ABOUT CONSUMERS OTHER THAN INFORMATION TYPICALLY ACQUIRED IN A FINANCIAL TRANSACTION CONDUCTED AT A RETAIL LIQUOR STORE.

(d) THE GENERAL ASSEMBLY SHALL ENACT AN EXCISE TAX TO BE LEVIED UPON MARIJUANA SOLD OR OTHERWISE TRANSFERRED BY A MARIJUANA CULTIVATION FACILITY TO A MARIJUANA PRODUCT MANUFACTURING FACILITY OR TO A RETAIL MARIJUANA STORE AT A RATE NOT TO EXCEED FIFTEEN PERCENT PRIOR TO JANUARY 1, 2017 AND AT A RATE TO BE DETERMINED BY THE GENERAL ASSEMBLY THEREAFTER, AND SHALL DIRECT THE DEPARTMENT TO ESTABLISH PROCEDURES FOR THE COLLECTION OF ALL TAXES LEVIED. PROVIDED, THE FIRST FORTY MILLION DOLLARS IN REVENUE RAISED ANNUALLY FROM ANY SUCH EXCISE TAX SHALL BE CREDITED TO THE PUBLIC SCHOOL CAPITAL CONSTRUCTION ASSISTANCE FUND CREATED BY ARTICLE 43.7 OF TITLE 22, C.R.S., OR ANY SUCCESSOR FUND DEDICATED TO A SIMILAR PURPOSE. PROVIDED FURTHER, NO SUCH EXCISE TAX SHALL BE LEVIED UPON MARIJUANA INTENDED FOR SALE AT MEDICAL MARIJUANA CENTERS PURSUANT TO SECTION 14 OF THIS ARTICLE AND THE COLORADO MEDICAL MARIJUANA CODE.

(e) NOT LATER THAN OCTOBER 1, 2013, EACH LOCALITY SHALL ENACT AN ORDINANCE OR REGULATION SPECIFYING THE ENTITY WITHIN THE LOCALITY THAT IS RESPONSIBLE FOR PROCESSING APPLICATIONS SUBMITTED FOR A LICENSE TO OPERATE A MARIJUANA ESTABLISHMENT WITHIN

THE BOUNDARIES OF THE LOCALITY AND FOR THE ISSUANCE OF SUCH LICENSES SHOULD THE ISSUANCE BY THE LOCALITY BECOME NECESSARY BECAUSE OF A FAILURE BY THE DEPARTMENT TO ADOPT REGULATIONS PURSUANT TO PARAGRAPH (a) OR BECAUSE OF A FAILURE BY THE DEPARTMENT TO PROCESS AND ISSUE LICENSES AS REQUIRED BY PARAGRAPH (g).

(f) A LOCALITY MAY ENACT ORDINANCES OR REGULATIONS, NOT IN CONFLICT WITH THIS SECTION OR WITH REGULATIONS OR LEGISLATION ENACTED PURSUANT TO THIS SECTION, GOVERNING THE TIME, PLACE, MANNER AND NUMBER OF MARIJUANA ESTABLISHMENT OPERATIONS; ESTABLISHING PROCEDURES FOR THE ISSUANCE, SUSPENSION, AND REVOCATION OF A LICENSE ISSUED BY THE LOCALITY IN ACCORDANCE WITH PARAGRAPH (h) OR (i), SUCH PROCEDURES TO BE SUBJECT TO ALL REQUIREMENTS OF ARTICLE 4 OF TITLE 24 OF THE COLORADO ADMINISTRATIVE PROCEDURE ACT OR ANY SUCCESSOR PROVISION; ESTABLISHING A SCHEDULE OF ANNUAL OPERATING, LICENSING, AND APPLICATION FEES FOR MARIJUANA ESTABLISHMENTS, PROVIDED, THE APPLICATION FEE SHALL ONLY BE DUE IF AN APPLICATION IS SUBMITTED TO A LOCALITY IN ACCORDANCE WITH PARAGRAPH (i) AND A LICENSING FEE SHALL ONLY BE DUE IF A LICENSE IS ISSUED BY A LOCALITY IN ACCORDANCE WITH PARAGRAPH (h) OR (i); AND ESTABLISHING CIVIL PENALTIES FOR VIOLATION OF AN ORDINANCE OR REGULATION GOVERNING THE TIME, PLACE, AND MANNER OF A MARIJUANA ESTABLISHMENT THAT MAY OPERATE IN SUCH LOCALITY. A LOCALITY MAY PROHIBIT THE OPERATION OF MARIJUANA CULTIVATION

FACILITIES, MARIJUANA PRODUCT MANUFACTURING FACILITIES, MARIJUANA TESTING FACILITIES, OR RETAIL MARIJUANA STORES THROUGH THE ENACTMENT OF AN ORDINANCE OR THROUGH AN INITIATED OR REFERRED MEASURE; PROVIDED, ANY INITIATED OR REFERRED MEASURE TO PROHIBIT THE OPERATION OF MARIJUANA CULTIVATION FACILITIES, MARIJUANA PRODUCT MANUFACTURING FACILITIES, MARIJUANA TESTING FACILITIES, OR RETAIL MARIJUANA STORES MUST APPEAR ON A GENERAL ELECTION BALLOT DURING AN EVEN NUMBERED YEAR.

(g) EACH APPLICATION FOR AN ANNUAL LICENSE TO OPERATE A MARIJUANA ESTABLISHMENT SHALL BE SUBMITTED TO THE DEPARTMENT. THE DEPARTMENT SHALL:

(I) BEGIN ACCEPTING AND PROCESSING APPLICATIONS ON OCTOBER 1, 2013;

(II) IMMEDIATELY FORWARD A COPY OF EACH APPLICATION AND HALF OF THE LICENSE APPLICATION FEE TO THE LOCALITY IN WHICH THE APPLICANT DESIRES TO OPERATE THE MARIJUANA ESTABLISHMENT;

(III) ISSUE AN ANNUAL LICENSE TO THE APPLICANT BETWEEN FORTY-FIVE AND NINETY DAYS AFTER RECEIPT OF AN APPLICATION UNLESS THE DEPARTMENT FINDS THE APPLICANT IS NOT IN COMPLIANCE WITH REGULATIONS ENACTED PURSUANT TO PARAGRAPH (a) OR THE DEPARTMENT IS NOTIFIED BY THE RELEVANT LOCALITY THAT THE APPLICANT IS NOT IN COMPLIANCE WITH ORDINANCES AND REGULATIONS MADE PURSUANT TO PARAGRAPH (f) AND IN EFFECT AT THE TIME OF APPLICATION, PROVIDED, WHERE A LOCALITY HAS ENACTED A NUMERICAL LIMIT ON THE NUMBER OF MARIJUANA

ESTABLISHMENTS AND A GREATER NUMBER OF APPLICANTS SEEK LICENSES, THE DEPARTMENT SHALL SOLICIT AND CONSIDER INPUT FROM THE LOCALITY AS TO THE LOCALITY'S PREFERENCE OR PREFERENCES FOR LICENSURE; AND

(IV) UPON DENIAL OF AN APPLICATION, NOTIFY THE APPLICANT IN WRITING OF THE SPECIFIC REASON FOR ITS DENIAL.

(h) IF THE DEPARTMENT DOES NOT ISSUE A LICENSE TO AN APPLICANT WITHIN NINETY DAYS OF RECEIPT OF THE APPLICATION FILED IN ACCORDANCE WITH PARAGRAPH (g) AND DOES NOT NOTIFY THE APPLICANT OF THE SPECIFIC REASON FOR ITS DENIAL, IN WRITING AND WITHIN SUCH TIME PERIOD, OR IF THE DEPARTMENT HAS ADOPTED REGULATIONS PURSUANT TO PARAGRAPH (a) AND HAS ACCEPTED APPLICATIONS PURSUANT TO PARAGRAPH (g) BUT HAS NOT ISSUED ANY LICENSES BY JANUARY 1, 2014, THE APPLICANT MAY RESUBMIT ITS APPLICATION DIRECTLY TO THE LOCALITY, PURSUANT TO PARAGRAPH (e), AND THE LOCALITY MAY ISSUE AN ANNUAL LICENSE TO THE APPLICANT. A LOCALITY ISSUING A LICENSE TO AN APPLICANT SHALL DO SO WITHIN NINETY DAYS OF RECEIPT OF THE RESUBMITTED APPLICATION UNLESS THE LOCALITY FINDS AND NOTIFIES THE APPLICANT THAT THE APPLICANT IS NOT IN COMPLIANCE WITH ORDINANCES AND REGULATIONS MADE PURSUANT TO PARAGRAPH (f) IN EFFECT AT THE TIME THE APPLICATION IS RESUBMITTED AND THE LOCALITY SHALL NOTIFY THE DEPARTMENT IF AN ANNUAL LICENSE HAS BEEN ISSUED TO THE APPLICANT. IF AN APPLICATION IS SUBMITTED TO A LOCALITY UNDER THIS PARAGRAPH, THE DEPARTMENT SHALL FORWARD TO THE LOCALITY THE APPLICATION FEE

PAID BY THE APPLICANT TO THE DEPARTMENT UPON REQUEST BY THE LOCALITY. A LICENSE ISSUED BY A LOCALITY IN ACCORDANCE WITH THIS PARAGRAPH SHALL HAVE THE SAME FORCE AND EFFECT AS A LICENSE ISSUED BY THE DEPARTMENT IN ACCORDANCE WITH PARAGRAPH (g) AND THE HOLDER OF SUCH LICENSE SHALL NOT BE SUBJECT TO REGULATION OR ENFORCEMENT BY THE DEPARTMENT DURING THE TERM OF THAT LICENSE. A SUBSEQUENT OR RENEWED LICENSE MAY BE ISSUED UNDER THIS PARAGRAPH ON AN ANNUAL BASIS ONLY UPON RESUBMISSION TO THE LOCALITY OF A NEW APPLICATION SUBMITTED TO THE DEPARTMENT PURSUANT TO PARAGRAPH (g). NOTHING IN THIS PARAGRAPH SHALL LIMIT SUCH RELIEF AS MAY BE AVAILABLE TO AN AGGRIEVED PARTY UNDER SECTION 24-4-104, C.R.S., OF THE COLORADO ADMINISTRATIVE PROCEDURE ACT OR ANY SUCCESSOR PROVISION.

(i) IF THE DEPARTMENT DOES NOT ADOPT REGULATIONS REQUIRED BY PARAGRAPH (a), AN APPLICANT MAY SUBMIT AN APPLICATION DIRECTLY TO A LOCALITY AFTER OCTOBER 1, 2013 AND THE LOCALITY MAY ISSUE AN ANNUAL LICENSE TO THE APPLICANT. A LOCALITY ISSUING A LICENSE TO AN APPLICANT SHALL DO SO WITHIN NINETY DAYS OF RECEIPT OF THE APPLICATION UNLESS IT FINDS AND NOTIFIES THE APPLICANT THAT THE APPLICANT IS NOT IN COMPLIANCE WITH ORDINANCES AND REGULATIONS MADE PURSUANT TO PARAGRAPH (f) IN EFFECT AT THE TIME OF APPLICATION AND SHALL NOTIFY THE DEPARTMENT IF AN ANNUAL LICENSE HAS BEEN ISSUED TO THE APPLICANT. A LICENSE ISSUED BY A LOCALITY IN ACCORDANCE WITH THIS PARAGRAPH SHALL HAVE THE SAME FORCE AND EFFECT AS A LICENSE

ISSUED BY THE DEPARTMENT IN ACCORDANCE WITH PARAGRAPH (g) AND THE HOLDER OF SUCH LICENSE SHALL NOT BE SUBJECT TO REGULATION OR ENFORCEMENT BY THE DEPARTMENT DURING THE TERM OF THAT LICENSE. A SUBSEQUENT OR RENEWED LICENSE MAY BE ISSUED UNDER THIS PARAGRAPH ON AN ANNUAL BASIS IF THE DEPARTMENT HAS NOT ADOPTED REGULATIONS REQUIRED BY PARAGRAPH (a) AT LEAST NINETY DAYS PRIOR TO THE DATE UPON WHICH SUCH SUBSEQUENT OR RENEWED LICENSE WOULD BE EFFECTIVE OR IF THE DEPARTMENT HAS ADOPTED REGULATIONS PURSUANT TO PARAGRAPH (a) BUT HAS NOT, AT LEAST NINETY DAYS AFTER THE ADOPTION OF SUCH REGULATIONS, ISSUED LICENSES PURSUANT TO PARAGRAPH (g).

(j) NOT LATER THAN JULY 1, 2014, THE GENERAL ASSEMBLY SHALL ENACT LEGISLATION GOVERNING THE CULTIVATION, PROCESSING AND SALE OF INDUSTRIAL HEMP.

**(6) Employers, driving, minors and control of property.**

(a) NOTHING IN THIS SECTION IS INTENDED TO REQUIRE AN EMPLOYER TO PERMIT OR ACCOMMODATE THE USE, CONSUMPTION, POSSESSION, TRANSFER, DISPLAY, TRANSPORTATION, SALE OR GROWING OF MARIJUANA IN THE WORKPLACE OR TO AFFECT THE ABILITY OF EMPLOYERS TO HAVE POLICIES RESTRICTING THE USE OF MARIJUANA BY EMPLOYEES.

(b) NOTHING IN THIS SECTION IS INTENDED TO ALLOW DRIVING UNDER THE INFLUENCE OF MARIJUANA OR DRIVING WHILE IMPAIRED BY MARIJUANA OR TO SUPERSEDE STATUTORY LAWS RELATED TO DRIVING UNDER THE INFLUENCE OF

MARIJUANA OR DRIVING WHILE IMPAIRED BY MARIJUANA, NOR SHALL THIS SECTION PREVENT THE STATE FROM ENACTING AND IMPOSING PENALTIES FOR DRIVING UNDER THE INFLUENCE OF OR WHILE IMPAIRED BY MARIJUANA.

(c) NOTHING IN THIS SECTION IS INTENDED TO PERMIT THE TRANSFER OF MARIJUANA, WITH OR WITHOUT REMUNERATION, TO A PERSON UNDER THE AGE OF TWENTY-ONE OR TO ALLOW A PERSON UNDER THE AGE OF TWENTY-ONE TO PURCHASE, POSSESS, USE, TRANSPORT, GROW, OR CONSUME MARIJUANA.

(d) NOTHING IN THIS SECTION SHALL PROHIBIT A PERSON, EMPLOYER, SCHOOL, HOSPITAL, DETENTION FACILITY, CORPORATION OR ANY OTHER ENTITY WHO OCCUPIES, OWNS OR CONTROLS A PROPERTY FROM PROHIBITING OR OTHERWISE REGULATING THE POSSESSION, CONSUMPTION, USE, DISPLAY, TRANSFER, DISTRIBUTION, SALE, TRANSPORTATION, OR GROWING OF MARIJUANA ON OR IN THAT PROPERTY.

**(7) Medical marijuana provisions unaffected.** NOTHING IN THIS SECTION SHALL BE CONSTRUED: (a) TO LIMIT ANY PRIVILEGES OR RIGHTS OF A MEDICAL MARIJUANA PATIENT, PRIMARY CAREGIVER, OR LICENSED ENTITY AS PROVIDED IN SECTION 14 OF THIS ARTICLE AND THE COLORADO MEDICAL MARIJUANA CODE; (b) TO PERMIT A MEDICAL MARIJUANA CENTER TO DISTRIBUTE MARIJUANA TO A PERSON WHO IS NOT A MEDICAL MARIJUANA PATIENT; (c) TO PERMIT A MEDICAL MARIJUANA CENTER TO PURCHASE MARIJUANA OR MARIJUANA PRODUCTS IN A MANNER OR FROM A SOURCE NOT AUTHORIZED UNDER THE COLORADO MEDICAL MARIJUANA

CODE; (d) TO PERMIT ANY MEDICAL MARIJUANA CENTER LICENSED PURSUANT TO SECTION 14 OF THIS ARTICLE AND THE COLORADO MEDICAL MARIJUANA CODE TO OPERATE ON THE SAME PREMISES AS A RETAIL MARIJUANA STORE.; OR (e) TO DISCHARGE THE DEPARTMENT, THE COLORADO BOARD OF HEALTH, OR THE COLORADO DEPARTMENT OF PUBLIC HEALTH AND ENVIRONMENT FROM THEIR STATUTORY AND CONSTITUTIONAL DUTIES TO REGULATE MEDICAL MARIJUANA PURSUANT TO SECTION 14 OF THIS ARTICLE AND THE COLORADO MEDICAL MARIJUANA CODE.

**(8) Self-executing, severability, conflicting provisions.** ALL PROVISIONS OF THIS SECTION ARE SELF-EXECUTING EXCEPT AS SPECIFIED HEREIN, ARE SEVERABLE, AND, EXCEPT WHERE OTHERWISE INDICATED IN THE TEXT, SHALL SUPERSEDE CONFLICTING STATE STATUTORY, LOCAL CHARTER, ORDINANCE, OR RESOLUTION, AND OTHER STATE AND LOCAL PROVISIONS.

**(9) Effective date.** UNLESS OTHERWISE PROVIDED BY THIS SECTION, ALL PROVISIONS OF THIS SECTION SHALL BECOME EFFECTIVE UPON OFFICIAL DECLARATION OF THE VOTE HEREON BY PROCLAMATION OF THE GOVERNOR, PURSUANT TO SECTION 1(4) OF ARTICLE V.

Several U.S. states currently allow the use of cannabis for qualified medical uses. Below is a chart of each state's medical marijuana laws for reference.

## Medical Marijuana State Law Overview

| State | Year Passed | How Passed (Yes Vote) | Fee | Possession Limit | Accepts other states' registry ID cards? |
|-------|-------------|------------------------|-----|------------------|------------------------------------------|
| Alaska | 1998 | Ballot Measure 8 (58%) | $25/$20 | 1 oz usable; 6 plants (3 mature, 3 immature) | unknown |
| Arizona | 2010 | Proposition 203 (50.13%) | $150/$75 | 2.5 oz usable; 0-12 plants$^2$ | Yes/possess No/purchase |
| California | 1996 | Proposition 215 (56%) | $66/$33 | 8 oz usable; 18 plants (6 mature, 12 immature)$^4$ | No |
| Colorado | 2000 | Ballot Amendment 20 (54%) | $90 | 2 oz usable; 6 plants (3 mature, 3 immature) | No |
| DC | 2010 | Amendment Act B18-622 (13-0 vote) | * | 2 oz dried; limits on other forms to be determined | unknown |
| Delaware | 2011 | Senate Bill 17 (27-14 House, 17-4 Senate) | ** | 6 oz usable | Yes |
| Hawaii | 2000 | Senate Bill 862 (32-18 House; 13-12 Senate) | $25 | 3 oz usable; 7 plants (3 mature, 4 immature) | No |

| State | Year | Bill | Fee | Amount | Insurance |
|---|---|---|---|---|---|
| **Maine** | 1999 | Ballot Question 2 (61%) | $100/$75 | 2.5 oz usable; 6 plants | Yes |
| **Michigan** | 2008 | Proposal 1 (63%) | $100/$25 | 2.5 oz usable; 12 plants | Yes |
| **Montana** | 2004 | Initiative 148 (62%) | $25/$10 | 1 oz usable; 6 plants | Yes |
| **Nevada** | 2000 | Ballot Question 9 (65%) | $150+ | 1 oz usable; 7 plants (3 mature, 4 immature) | No |
| **New Jersey** | 2010 | Senate Bill 119 (48-14 House; 25-13 Senate) | $200/$20 | 2 oz usable | unknown |
| **New Mexico** | 2007 | Senate Bill 523 (36-31 House; 32-3 Senate) | $0 | 6 oz usable; 16 plants (4 mature, 12 immature) | No |
| **Oregon** | 1998 | Ballot Measure 67 (55%) | $100/$20 | 24 oz usable; 24 plants (6 mature, 18 immature) | No |
| **Rhode Island** | 2006 | Senate Bill 0710 (52-10 House; 33-1 Senate) | $75/$10 | 2.5 oz usable; 12 plants | Yes |
| **Vermont** | 2004 | Senate Bill 76 (22-7) HB 645 (82-59) | $50 | 2 oz usable; 9 plants (2 mature, 7 immature) | No |
| **Washington** | 1998 | Initiative 692 (59%) | *** | 24 oz usable; 15 plants | No |

*Additional Source- ProCon.org*

# LIST OF PLACES TO PURCHASE MARIJUANA IN THE STATE OF COLORADO

1617 WAZEE STREET, LLC
1617 Wazee Street, Unit B, Denver CO 80202

3-D DENVER'S DISCREET DISPENSARY LLC
4305 Brighton Boulevard, Denver CO 80216

4625 EAST COLFAX, LLC
4625 East Colfax Avenue, Denver CO 80220

5110 RACE, LLC
5110 Race Street, Denver CO 80216

5280 MEDS/WELLNESS
1321 Elati Street, Denver CO 80204

A CUT OFF THE TOP MEDICAL MARIJUANA, LLC
2059 West 9th Avenue, Unit A, Denver CO 80204

ADVANCED MEDICAL ALTERNATIVES LLC
1269-71 Elati Street, Denver CO 80204

ALCC LLC
2748 West Alameda Avenue, Denver CO 80219

ALPENGLOW BOTANICALS, LLC
1805 Airport Road, #B1C & B1B, Breckenridge CO 80424

ALPINE WELLNESS LLC
300 West Colorado Avenue, Telluride CO 81435

ALTERNATIVE MEDICAL SUPPLIES LLC
9 Karlann Drive, Black Hawk CO 80422

ALTERNATIVE MEDICINE ON CAPITOL HILL
1301 Marion Street, Denver CO 80218

ALTERNATIVE MEDICINE ON THE MALL, LLC
910 16th Street, Suite 805, Denver CO 80202

ALTITUDE WELLNESS CENTER LLC
3435 South Yosemite Street, Suite 200, Denver CO 80231

ANNIE'S TOBACCO EMPORIUM, LLC
135 Nevada Street, Central City CO 80427

AREN & DAVE'S DREAM, LLC
1402 Argentine Street, Georgetown CO 80444

BIOENERGETIC HEALING CENTER LLC
842 North Summit Boulevard, #13, Frisco CO 80443

BOTANACARE LLC
11450 Cherokee Street, #A5, A6, A7, Northglenn CO 80234

BOTANICO, INC.
3054 Larimer Street, Denver CO 80205

BRECKENRIDGE CANNABIS CLUB LLC
226 South Main Street, Breckenridge CO 80424

BUD MED HEALTH CENTERS, LLC
2517 Sheridan Boulevard, Edgewater CO 80214

CAM CORP
2394 South Broadway, Denver CO 80210

CANNABIS KING, LLC
1131 West Custer Place, Unit A, Denver CO 80223

CAREGIVERS FOR LIFE LLC
310 Saint Paul Street, Denver CO 80206

CHOICE ORGANICS, INC.
813 Smithfield Drive, Units C & D, Fort Collins CO 80524

CITI-MED, LLC
1640 East Evans Avenue, Denver CO 80210

CJJ SERVICES, LLC
5885 East Evans Avenue, Denver CO 80222

CLOUD 9 CAREGIVERS
2506 6th Avenue, Garden City CO 80631

CMED, LLC
615 Buggy Circle, Unit D, Carbondale CO 81623

CO-AGRONOMICS LLC
2020 South Broadway, Denver CO 80210

COLORADO CARE FACILITY, INC.
5130 East Colfax, Denver CO 80220

COLORADO HEALTH CONSULTANTS, LLC
4690 North Brighton Boulevard, Denver CO 80216

COLORADO PRODUCT SERVICES
580 Main Street, Suite 300, Carbondale CO 81623

COLORADO WELLNESS CENTERS LLC
2490 West 2nd Avenue, Denver CO 80223

COLORADO WELLNESS INC
2057 South Broadway, Denver CO 80210

COMPASSIONATE CARE GIVERS, INC.
1201 20th Street, Denver CO 80205

COMPASSIONATE CARE GIVERS, INC.
1233 West Alameda Avenue, Denver CO 80223

COMPASSIONATE CARE GIVERS, INC.
1538 Wazee Street, Denver CO 80202

COOPER MASON VENTURES LLC
520 East Cooper Avenue, LL2, Aspen CO 81611

CURE MEDICAL PHARM INC
990 West 6th Avenue, #5, Denver CO 80204

DELTA 9 ALTERNATIVE MEDICINE LLC
2262 South Broadway, Denver CO 80210

DENCO, LLC
3460 Park Avenue West, Unit D, Denver CO 80216

DENVER DISPENSARY, LLC
4975 Vasquez Boulevard, Denver CO 80216

DENVER RELIEF LLC
1 Broadway, #A-150, Denver CO 80203

DGS, INC.
1881 South Broadway, Denver CO 80210

DISCOUNT MEDICAL MARIJUANA
2028 East Colfax Avenue, Denver CO 80206

DISCOUNT MEDICAL MARIJUANA
970 Lincoln Street, Denver CO 80203

DKC, LLC
2615 Welton Street, Denver CO 80205

DOCTORS ORDERS, LLC
1406 West 38th Avenue, Denver CO 80211

EVERGREEN APOTHECARY, LLC
1568 South Broadway, Denver CO 80210

EVER-GREEN HERBAL REMEDIES, LLC
15 Colorado Boulevard, Unit A, Idaho Springs CO 80452

FLAVORED ESSENTIALS, LLC
3955 Oneida Street, Denver CO 80207

F-SQUARED INDUSTRIES, LLC
330 South Dayton, Denver CO 80247

**GANJA GOURMET, LLC**
1810 South Broadway, Denver CO 80210

**GG MERCANTILE**
1332 South Cherokee Street, Denver CO 80223

**GOLDEN MEDS, INC.**
4620 Peoria Street, Denver CO 80239

**GREEN GRASS, LLC**
440 Lawrence Street, Central City CO 80427

**GREENER PASTURE COMPASSION CENTER, LLC**
5101 East Colfax Avenue, Denver CO 80220

**GREENWERKZ, LLC**
5840 West 25th Avenue, Denver CO 80214

**HCH2, LLC**
40 South Main Street, Alma CO 80420

**HERBAL ALTERNATIVES LLC**
2568 South Broadway, Denver CO 80210

**HERB'S NEST, LLC**
3900 East 48th Avenue, Denver CO 80216

**HIGH COUNTRY SUPPLY, LLC**
1178 South Kalamath Street, Denver CO 80223

**HIGHLANDS WELLNESS CENTER, LLC**
3460 West 32nd Avenue, Denver CO 80211

HOLLY MEDICINAL SERVICES, LLC
3888 East Mexico Avenue, Suite 110, Denver CO 80210

IVITA WELLNESS LLC
3980 Franklin Street, Denver CO 80205

IVITA WELLNESS LLC
1660 Pearl Street, Denver CO 80203

JGB VENTURES LLC
3835 Elm Street, Unit B & C, Denver CO 80207

JOIS LLC
3700 West Quincy Avenue, #3702, Denver CO 80236

JS INVESTMENTS
401 16th Street, Denver CO 80202

KAYAK CORPORATION
1325 South Inca Street, Suite A, Denver CO 80223

KAZIMER, LLC
1450 South Santa Fe Drive, Unit 102, Denver CO 80223

LIGHTSHADE LABS LLC
3950 Holly Street, Denver CO 80207

LIVE GREEN CONSULTING, LLC
4000 Morrison Road, Denver CO 80219

MAGNA MARKETING, INC.
20 East 9th Avenue, Denver CO 80203

MARISOL THERAPEUTICS, LLC
922 East Kimble Drive, Pueblo CO 81007

MAYFLOWER GROUP, LLC
1736 Downing Street, Denver CO 80218

MEDICINAL WELLNESS CENTER LLC
5430 West 44th Avenue, Denver CO 80212

MEDICINAL WELLNESS CENTER LLC
6359 East Evans Avenue, Denver CO 80222

MEDICINE MAN PRODUCTION CORPORATION
4750 Nome Street, Unit B, Denver CO 80239

METRO CANNABIS INC
8151 East Colfax Avenue, Denver CO 80220

METROPOLIS MEDICAL, LLC
4600 Ironton Street, Denver CO 80239

MGI INC
4125 Elati Street, Denver CO 80216

MILAGRO WELLNESS HEALING LLC
1181 County Road 308, Dumont CO 80436

MILE HIGH MEDICAL CANNABIS, LLC
1705 North Federal Boulevard, Denver CO 80204

MILE HIGH MEDICAL, LLC
2042 Arapahoe Street, Denver CO 80205

MILE HIGH THERAPEUTIC NETWORK LLC
1568 South Federal Boulevard, Denver CO 80219

MMD OF COLORADO LLC
2609 Walnut Street, Denver CO 80205

MMD OF COLORADO LLC
3954 Williams Street, Denver CO 80205

MMST, LLC
1724 South Broadway, Denver CO 80210

NATURAL CHOICE CO-OP
2835 Downhill Plaza, Unit 603, Steamboat Springs CO 80487

NATURAL HIGH LLC
1013 Poplar Street, Unit One, Leadville CO 80461

NATURES CURE III, LLC
1500 East Colfax Avenue, Denver CO 80218

NATURES CURE LLC
4283 West Florida Avenue, Denver CO 80219
NATURE'S HERBS & WELLNESS CENTER
522 27th Street, Greeley CO 80631

NEW WORLD ALTERNATIVE HEALTHCARE LLC
135 South Spruce Street, Telluride CO 81435

NORTH FEDERAL, LLC
74 Federal Boulevard, Denver CO 80219

NORTHERN LIGHTS NATURALS, LLC
2045 Sheridan Boulevard, Suite B, Denver CO 80214

NUTRITIONAL ELEMENTS, INC.
2777 South Colorado Boulevard, Denver CO 80222

O LIMITED
1 West First Street, Unit 1D, Nederland CO 80466

ORGANIC GREENS, INC.
1620 Market Street, Suite 5W, Denver CO 80202

ORGANIX, LLC
1795 Airport Road, A2, Breckenridge CO 80424

PAIN MANAGEMENT OF GOVERNORS PARK, LLC
745 East 6th Avenue, Denver CO 80203

PATIENTS CHOICE OF COLORADO, LLC
2251 South Broadway, Denver CO 80210

PHYSICIAN PREFERRED PRODUCTS LLC
2100 East 112th Avenue, #5 Northglenn CO 80233

PUEBLO WEST ORGANICS LLC
609 East Enterprise Drive, Suite 130, Pueblo CO 81007

RIVERROCK LLC
4935 York Street, Denver CO 80216

RK ENTERPRISES LTD
2730 Downhill Plaza, #106, Steamboat Springs CO 80487

**ROCKY MOUNTAIN CAREGIVERS INC**
2601 West Alameda Avenue, Denver CO 80219

**ROCKY MOUNTAIN FARMACY INC**
4095 Jackson Street, Denver CO 80216

**SENSE OF HEALING LLC**
1005 Federal Boulevard, Denver CO 80204

**SERENE WELLNESS LLC**
13 East Park Avenue, Empire CO 80438

**STONE T.M.C., LLC**
4820 Morrison Road, Denver CO 80219

**SUMMIT WELLNESS LLC**
2117 Larimer Street, #1, Denver CO 80205

**SUNRISE SOLUTIONS, LLC**
43 Main Street, Bailey CO 80421

**SWEETWATER PARTNERS, LLC**
330 East Colfax Avenue, Denver CO 80203

**TELLURIDE GREEN ROOM LLC**
250 South Fir Street, #5 & #6, Telluride CO 81435

**TETRA HYDRO CENTER LLC**
9206 East Hampden Avenue, Denver CO 80231

THE GIVING TREE OF DENVER LLC
2707 West 38th Avenue, Denver CO 80211

THE GREEN SOLUTION LLC
470 Malley Drive, Northglenn CO 80233

THE GREEN SOLUTION LLC
4400 Grape Street, Denver CO 80216

THE GREENER SIDE CAREGIVING AND WELLNESS LLC
3321 Interstate 25 South, Pueblo CO 81004

THE HERBAL CENTER, LLC
1909 South Broadway, Denver CO 80210

THE HERBAL CURE LLC
985 South Logan Street, Denver CO 80209

THE KINE MINE LLC
2818 Colorado Boulevard, Idaho Springs CO 80452

THE PURPLE DRAGON, LLC
2243 Federal Boulevard, Denver CO 80211
THE TEA POT, LLC
2008 Federal Boulevard, Denver CO 80211

TIMBERLINE HERBAL CLINIC AND WELLNESS CENTER, LLC
3995 East 50th Avenue, Denver CO 80216

TMED LLC
3944 North High Street, Denver CO 80205

**TREATMENTS UNLIMITED, LLC**
6858 East Evans Avenue, Denver CO 80224

**TZ FINANCIAL, LLC**
191 Blue River Parkway, Silverthorne CO 80498

**URBAN CANNABIS, LLC**
2383 South Downing Street, Denver CO 80210

**WALKING RAVEN, LLC**
2001 South Broadway, Denver CO 80210

**WANNA LLC**
183 West Alameda Avenue, Denver CO 80223

**WDG, INC.**
5926 East Colfax Avenue, Denver CO 80220

**WESTERN REMEDIES LLC**
777 Canosa Court, #102, Denver CO 80204

## The History of Medical Marijuana

Although the use of Cannabis dates back centuries to pretty much the beginning of history, California was the first state in the U.S. to legalize marijuana use for medical reasons. Passed by California voters, that act, Proposition 215 was titled, the Compassionate Use Act. The person who was behind this is longtime activist and San Francisco resident, Dennis Peron. Peron led several campaigns in San Francisco to make cannabis obtainable to AIDS patients during the AIDS epidemic.

Dennis Peron successfully lobbied two Propositions within San Francisco's government which made enforcing marijuana laws against sick people in the city a low priority. Peron would then go on to open the very first public medical marijuana dispensary in U.S. history, The San Francisco Cannabis Buyers Club.

Peron got his start way back in San Francisco in 1969 selling pot after returning from the Vietnam War. Up through the 1970's he ran the Big Top marijuana supermarket from his home in San Francisco's predominantly gay, Castro District.

In 1978 Peron created Proposition W which directed the district attorney to stop arresting people for possessing,

Dennis Peron, Circa 1996

transferring, or growing marijuana. Though it was passed by 56% of the electorate, it was never implemented by the city administration.

In 1991 Peron created Proposition P which made enforcement of laws against medical marijuana the city's lowest priority. It passed by 79%.

In 1993 he opened the Church Street Compassion Center in the Castro District.

In 1995 he opened the San Francisco Cannabis Buyers Club at 1444 Market Street where the medical marijuana movement and Proposition 215 were born.

In 1996 he co-authored The Compassionate Use Act of 1996 and organized the signature drive that put Proposition 215 on the ballot.

The club continued its operation uninterrupted by law enforcement for a couple years before Peron lobbied to put Proposition 215 on the state's ballot. Proposition 215, also called "the Compassionate Use Act" allowed those qualified access to medical marijuana and a guarantee that they would be safe from prosecution.

*True American Hero,*

*Dennis Peron*

Around this time the club started to get a lot of media attention. TV crews from all across the country started reporting on Peron's efforts and our freely distributing medical marijuana to the clubs thousands of members. This eventually caught the attention of then California Attorney General, Dan Lungren. Lungren made Peron a priority and led a raid on the club. all

No arrests were made but Lungren was criticized by many all the Way to the White House. Many allege Lungren's raid was politically motivated and was only days prior to the GOP Convention. It successfully closed the club temporarily by court order.

Inside the original San Francisco Cannabis Buyers Club

To have had the opportunity to work with Dennis through all this was the experience of a lifetime, and every medical marijuana patient needs to recognize that Dennis Peron was the person behind not only California, but every state that has now adopted laws protecting patients.

The club was home to a great number of patients

After Prop 215 passed, dispensaries slowly started to pop up. Two others opened before 215 even passed, one by my friend, Jeff Jones called the Oakland Cannabis Buyers Club and the other was the Santa Cruz Buyers Club. Jeff's membership shot up over 600% after our club was raided just in that first month.

In April, 2010, Dennis suffered a stroke at his home in San Francisco. Dennis is now retired from the industry and owns an awesome bed & breakfast in San Francisco's, Castro District. He occasionally teaches at Oaksterdam University in Oakland and appears as a speaker and celebrity guest at events all over the world.

## Methods of Ingestion

Smoking is the most common form of ingesting marijuana. THC is inhaled as a smoke and rapidly reaches the users bloodstream, usually within seconds. In less than a minute it reaches the receptors in the brain. Incineration of marijuana is done in the form of hand rolled marijuana cigarettes, commonly referred to as "joints" or by smoking using a pipe or device known as a water pipe or "bong". Users can also use a device called a vaporizer.

## VAPORIZER

Vaporizers heat marijuana to a temperature just under the point of combustion. At this point medically active resins begin to evaporate without burning or smoke. The vapor is then inhaled. Many people prefer this relatively new way to ingest marijuana because the effects are just as quick as burning but the harmful tars and chemicals which exist in marijuana smoke are avoided.

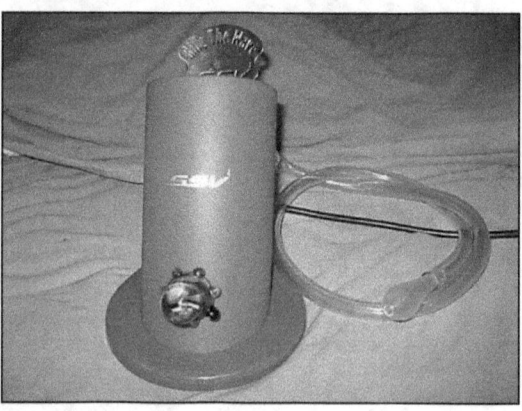

Pictured above, a vaporizer unit used for ingesting marijuana

## JOINTS

Joints are hand rolled marijuana cigarettes. They are smoked just like a cigarette. One end is ignited and smoke is drawn by the user sucking on the unlit end. Cigarette papers are readily available at most any convenience store or gas station. Other common slang names associated with joints include doobie, blunt, spliff, fatty, jay, etc

## PIPES

Pipes are a popular way to ingest marijuana and are readily available at smoke shops, through the internet, even from street vendors. The typical pipe is made of high quality blown glass. Pipes are available in a wide variety of styles and construction including metal and wood.

## WATERPIPES AND BONGS

Waterpipes work by drawing the smoke through a reservoir or water. This acts to cool the smoke making smoking from a waterpipe a much smoother smoke. The water also removes other particles from the smoke, including a small amount of THC.

A bong is a different creature although smoke is still drawn through a reservoir of water or water/ice mix. Bongs are usually constructed of a plastic or glass tube like chamber. Smoke enters the chamber by passing through water and a small hole on the side of the bong, often referred to as a "carburetor hole" is released allowing a large amount of smoke to be quickly inhaled by the user.

## TINCTURES

Tincture is a concentrated extract of marijuana in an alcohol, oil, or glycerol base. Tinctures are potent and safe herbal medicines, commonly found in health food stores and everything from St Johns Root to Valirum Root is available. Cannabis tincture is based on the same theory. A patient applies the droplets under the tongue. The tincture is then absorbed through the mucus membranes and goes directly into the patients' bloodstream, bypassing the liver altogether.

Effects of cannabis tinctures usually are felt within five minutes and develop into an effect much like inhaled THC.

Tincture is produced by soaking parts of the marijuana plant in a base which extracts the THC and other useful cannabinoids, separating them from the plant material and dissolving them into an alcohol or glycerin base.

## CAPSULES

Sometimes referred to as "maripills" marijuana pills are easy to make and quite effective. For people who find smoking unpleasant, and are looking for an alternative. Many prefer the high from oral ingestion compared to that produced from smoking. Studies have shown that cannabis has stronger analgesic and anti-inflammatory qualities when eaten. This is also a discreet way to have access to your medicine on trains, planes, or in public without firing up. Unlike the unpredictability of dosages with cannabis edibles, the dosage in capsules can be regulated and maintained.

Marijuana capsules take effect anywhere from 30 to 90 minutes after ingesting, faster on an empty stomach, and the effects generally last between 5 and 7 hours but medicinal benefits may continue for 24 hours.

Capsules are made from processing finely ground bud and leaf, which is heated in oil to make the ingredients more potent. Some patients just use high grade trim leaves from their garden. The ingredients are then put into empty gelatin capsules ready for consumption.

## FOOD (edibles)

The effect of THC that is prepared and ingested as food and the effect of THC from smoke are quite different. When

THC is absorbed through the stomach it is processed through the liver before reaching the brain. The liver converts THC to 11-hydroxy-THC, which may actually be a bit more psychoactive than THC which is smoked. Therefore, smoking and eating create two distinctive separate effects.

It takes longer to feel the effects of THC which is eaten, but its effects have been reported to last longer.

There is certainly an endless variety of edibles out there for you to choose from ranging from lollipops, hard candies and taffy to traditional brownies. There are now even cannabis sodas on the market.

Cooking with cannabis is also a common way of ingestion. This includes the use of ingredients like cannabis butter or oil or finely ground cannabis. Cannabis leaves and clippings "shake" is commonly used in food preparation. There are endless cannabis recipes all over the internet and in books for you to try.

Be responsible- make sure to take the proper precautions to make sure that nobody accidently eats your food. Clearly label your medicated foods and ensure they are secure, especially anywhere where children may have access to them, like a refrigerator.

Oral consumption is a popular way to take cannabis, especially with people who are sensitive to smoke, or want to avoid the presence of a marijuana smoke odor, or people who need to medicate discreetly. Many as I mentioned previously, like that high that oral ingestion produces. When eating marijuana, the dose can be hard to predict. Oral consumption is a great way to get the most out of lower grade marijuana.

*IMPORTANT NOTE: Make sure your edibles are clearly marked with the amount of THC ingredient; otherwise law enforcement will charge you with the entire weight of the edible.*

## TOPICAL SOLUTIONS/OINTMENTS

Evidence suggests that cannabis is effective for various topical uses. Many new products are popping up in dispensaries that are in a lotion/ointment or a balm or oil form. These products can be used to provide relief for localized pains. They are generally easy to create using skin friendly bases such as coconut oil, almond oil, aloe vera, or even olive oil.

It is advised to spot test a product before using liberally if it is the first time you are using it. This is done by placing a small amount on an area on your skin approximately the size of a dime.  Observe the area for any allergic reaction or rash.

A balm is made by taking beeswax and mixing with a cannabis oil base.

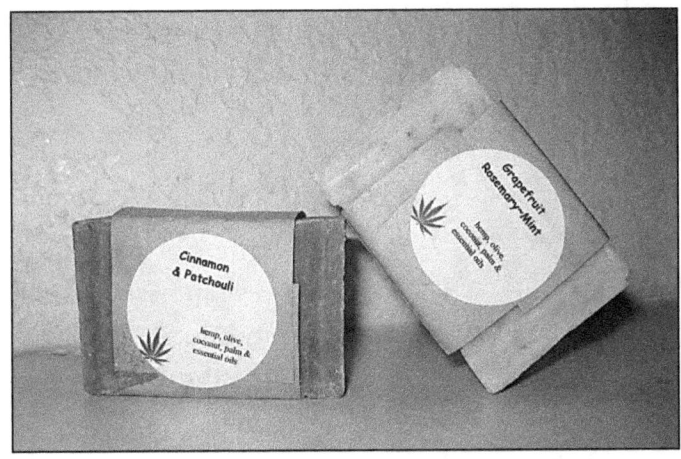

Cannabis (Hemp) infused soaps are popular

## BEAUTY PRODUCTS

As more people discover the highly beneficial properties of Hemp, Hemp based products are beginning to become more readily available to consumers.  Products such as soap, shampoo, lip balm, cuticle oil, lotions, and even washcloths.

**Lip Balm**

**Nail Polish Hardner**

There are countless
Hemp based
products
on the
market.

**Sun Tan Oil**

**USE OF HEMP BEAUTY CARE PRODUCTS WILL NOT CAUSE
FALSE DRUG TEST POSITIVE**

# Varieties of cannabis

There are a wide variety of marijuana strains currently available in dispensaries and directly from local farmers. Varieties are available in ready to smoke form and often in plant form as a "clone". Clones are planted and if properly cared for grow into full size cannabis plants. The growing stage is often referred to as the "vegetative stage". When the season changes or lighting times are shortened significantly, the plant senses this and begins its "bloom stage" producing buds. At the peak of development in this stage, the plant is harvested and usually produces between 16 and 24 ounces of useable bud. Clipping and leaves can be used for cooking and making tincture. Now that we've covered the full life span of a clone. Let's get back to our main subject.

Experienced growers are able to routinely cross-breed these various varieties to produce new hybrid varieties. So, there is no way I could list the wide scale of strains that are out there.

Technically there are three popular varieties of cannabis, Sativa, Indica, and Kush.

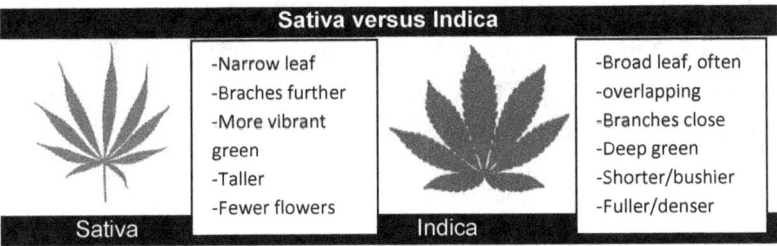

| Sativa versus Indica | | |
|---|---|---|
| Sativa | -Narrow leaf<br>-Braches further<br>-More vibrant green<br>-Taller<br>-Fewer flowers | Indica -Broad leaf, often<br>-overlapping<br>-Branches close<br>-Deep green<br>-Shorter/bushier<br>-Fuller/denser |

## SATIVA

Sativa plants can be found pretty much all over the world. There are potent varieties of Sativa that have origins in Columbia, Mexico, Panama, and Nigeria. Because Sativa originates in areas which have long season's it requires more time to produce.

Leaves on Sativa plants tend to be long and narrow, and the plants tend to grow very tall outdoors. Buds are long and semi-thick.

Buds are sweet smelling and produce a smooth smoke. The high produced by Sativa has been described as dreamy, psychedelic. Some claim the high makes them more creative and spacey.

## INDICA

The origins of the Indica strain can be traced back to Central Asia. Indica strains and its sub-strain Kush mature quickly. Their plants have short, compact branches. Their leaves are dark green and short and wide. Buds are tight and wide and can become long. Their distinctive odor is very pungent, especially in the budding stage.

The high produced from ingesting this strain is a very heavy, relaxing social high.

Based on my personal experience, Jamaican Indica is an excellent example of high quality indica cannabis.

## KUSH

Kush is a member of the Indica strain. Kush is sometimes also referred to as "Afghani". Kush originates from the Hindu-Kush Mountains where it has been consistently cultivated for thousands of years. This sweet smelling plant is short and squat in appearance. Some forms of Kush are a hybrid cross between Indica and Sativa strains.

Hindu Kush strains were brought to the United States in the mid-to-late 1970s and have been popular since.

O.G. Kush bud

### URINE

Urinalysis is the most common test type and used by federally mandated drug testing programs and is considered the gold standard of drug testing. Urine based tests have been upheld in most courts for more than 30 years.

In urine tests, THC is detectable 2 to 7 days, after heavy or chronic use and/or users with high body fat cannabis remains detectable in urine for 30 days or more. While this is true in some cases, studies have shown that detection times of 30+ days are actually quite rare, even for chronic users subjected to tests with lower than normal cutoffs. Under the typical 50 ng/mL cutoff for THC an occasional or one-off user would be very unlikely to test positive beyond 3–4 days since the last use, and a chronic user would be unlikely to test positive much beyond 7 days. The most likely maximum times are 7 days and 21 days, respectively. However every individual is different, and detection times can vary due to metabolism or other factors.

### HAIR

THC can remain detectable in hair strains for up to 90 days. A hair sample is cut close to the scalp and 80 to 120 strands of hair are needed for the test. In the absence of hair on the head, body hair can be used as an acceptable substitute.

One study has shown that THC does not readily deposit inside epithelial cells so it is possible for cosmetic and other forms of adulteration to reduce the amount of testable cannabinoids within a hair sample.

There are some shampoo's on the market that claim to eliminate THC from hair.  There is also a shampoo that was designed for people who spend a lot of time swimming in chlorinated pools that I understand is quite effective.

## SALIVA

THC can remain detectable in saliva for anywhere between two and twenty four hours.  THC may only be detectable for less than 12 hours in most cases.  Saliva tests are poorly sensitive to THC and detection times can really pretty much vary considerably based on the cutoffs used. In most  cases drug use may only be detectable for a few hours.

Adulteration products are readily available to avoid saliva detection.

## BLOOD

The times for detection of THC in blood is roughly 2 to 3 days for light use and up to 2 weeks in heavy or chronic users.  Depending on how much marijuana was consumed, it can usually be detected in blood tests within six hours of consumption. After six hours has passed, the concentration of marijuana in the blood decreases significantly. In most cases it generally disappears completely after 22 hours. This greatly depends on whether actual THC or THC metabolites are being tested for. Metabolites have a far greater detection time.

**Secondhand exposure will cause you to fail? FALSE**

This legend is technically true but highly misleading. According to a U.S. Army study, the amount of secondhand cannabis smoke needed to cause a false positive result (failure) is quite large indeed, and would require being sealed in an unventilated car or small room filled with marijuana smokers for several hours.

Hair testing, however, is a different matter, Though for cannabis, typically only metabolites (produced by the body and thus not found in smoke) are tested rather than THC, so failure is unlikely to result from non-extreme passive exposure.

**Ibuprofen causes false positives for THC? MAYBE**

While this was true in the past, newer versions of the EMIT bioassay are much less sensitive to ibuprofen (Advil, Motrin, etc.), and this has become relatively uncommon as of 1998, at least in the United States. However, abnormally high doses of ibuprofen can still potentially cause a false positive in some cases. Nonetheless, this no longer works as an alibi for THC since GC/MS can now distinguish between the two.

# Common Marijuana Strains & Their Characteristics

| Abr. | Strain | Origin | Med. Use | Effect |
|---|---|---|---|---|
| 707 | 707 Headband | H | nausea | inspired |
| A10 | A-10 | I | stress | creative/ elated |
| AG | Acapulco Gold | H | insomnia | uplifting/relaxed |
| AT | Accidental Tourist | H | pain | euphoric/incense |
| A1 | Afghani #1 | H | pain/spasm | Hashy/potent |
| Abr | Afgahni Bullrider | I | appetite | lazy/ blissful |
| Abb | Afghan Big Bud | H | migraine | joyous /up |
| Ad | Afghan Diesel | H | stress | euphoric/up |
| Afk | Afghan Kush | I | stress/appetite | lethargic |
| Afg | Afghani | I | stress | lazy/ blissful |
| Afy | Afghooey | H | stress | exhilarated / cheery |
| Afg | Afgoo | I | pain | euphoric/lazy |
| Afw | Afwreck | H | anxiety | cheerful |
| Ago | Agent Orange | H | appetite | happy/ chatty |
| Ak | AK-47 | H | stress | lethargic /euphoric |
| A48 | AK-48 | H | stress | uplifting/ inspired |
| ATF | Alaskan TF | S | PMS | cerebral/uplifting |
| Alk | Alien Kush | I | nausea | creative/ cheerful |
| Alo | Aloha | S | anxiety | up/euphoric |
| Alo | Alohaberry | H | stress | drive / absorbed |
| Amb | Ambrosia | H | anxiety | focus/uplifting |
| Ame | Amethyst | H | stress | lazy/ elated |
| Amh | Amnesia Haze | H | stress | euphoric/creative |
| An | Anesthesia | I | stress | lazy/happy |
| Apo | Apollo 11 | H | stress | exhilarated /up |
| A13 | Apollo 13 | S | energy | creative/clear |
| Apl | Apple Kush | H | anxiety | euphoric/creative |
| Ag | Arabian Gold | S | insomnia | euphoric/happy |
| Arj | Arjan's Strawberry Haze | S | pain | blissful /creative |
| Atn | Atomic Northern Lights | H | migraine | aroused/uppity |
| Atr | A-Train | H | appetite | lazy/happy |
| At | Australian Blue | H | nausea | strong/stoney |
| Ava | Avalon | H | appetite | tingly/up |
| Bna | Banana Diesel | H | appetite | focused/giggly |

67

| Abr. | Strain | Origin | Med. Use | Effect |
|---|---|---|---|---|
| Bk | Banana Kush | I | stress | euphoric/lazy |
| Bcr | BC Roadkill | H | anxiety | giggles/creative |
| BC | BC Sweet Tooth | H | anxiety | up/euphoric |
| Bd | Belladonna | S | insomnia | drowsy /relaxed |
| Brk | Berkeley | S | nausea | up/creative |
| Bb | Big Bud | H | appetite | lazy/uppity |
| Bbc | Big Budda Cheese | H | stress | up/creative |
| BCH | Big Cheese | H | asthma | relaxed/creative |
| Bgw | Big Wreck | H | migraine | up/lazy |
| Bdh | Black Dhalia | H | pain | tingly/ engrossed |
| Bkd | Black Diesel | S | pain | creative/euphoric |
| Bld | Black Domina | H | stress | happy/creative |
| Bj | Black Jack | H | pain | happy/up |
| Blk | Black Label Kush | I | insomnia | lazy/cheerful |
| BmK | Black Magic Kush | H | insomnia | tired/relaxed |
| Blw | Black Widow | H | appetite | euphoric/joyful |
| Bhp | Blackberry Hashplant | I | pain | euphoric/ lethargic |
| Bbk | Blackberry Kush | I | stress | lazy/tired |
| Blc | Blockhead | H | appetite | giggles/euphoric |

## The Hash Plant

A very potent Indica strain
that produces a narcotic like
high with a distinctive
lavender smell and
incense like taste

| Bbu | Blue Bayou | S | migraine | up/creative |
|---|---|---|---|---|
| Chz | Blue Cheese | H | stress | euphoric/ lethargic |
| Blc | Blue Crack | H | pain | uppity/euphoric |
| Bdr | Blue Dragon | H | anxiety | creative/up |

| Abr. | Strain | Origin | Med. Use | Effect |
|------|--------|--------|----------|--------|
| Bd | Blue Dream | H | stress | euphoric/creative |
| Bh | Blue Hammer | H | pain | trippy/euphoric |
| BMr | Blue Moon Rocks | H | mood | resinous/creeper |
| Blu | Blue Satellite | S | stress | uppity/talkative |
| Bu2 | Blue Satellite #2 | H | mood | cerebral/happy |
| Bth | Blue Thunder | H | stress | body buzz/focused |
| Bt | Blue Train | H | appetite | munchies/happy |
| Bw | Blue Widow | I | pain | euphoric/up |
| Bry | Blueberry | H | stress | joyful/euphoric |
| BAK | Blueberry AK | S | anxiety | rush/giggly |
| Bhz | Blueberry Haze | H | stress | uplifted/joyful |
| Bh | Blueberry Headband | H | stress | creative/energy |
| Bk | Blueberry Kush | I | anxiety | euphoric/energy |
| Bro | Broke Diesel | H | migraine | trippy/happy |
| Bhs | Bubble Hash | H | insomnia | sedative |
| Bbk | Bubble Kush | H | pain | potent/heavy |
| Bk | Bubba Kush | I | pain | tired/laidback |
| Bog | Bubba OG | I | stress | lazy/euphoric |
| Bg | Bubble Gum | H | anxiety | trippy/joyful |
| Bbr | Bubbleberry | H | stress | lazy/joyful |
| Bub | Bubblegun | H | appetite | creative/laidback |
| Bus | Buddha's Sister | I | pain | trippy/uppity |
| Buk | Burmese Kush | H | anxiety | clear/focused |
| Bsc | Butterscotch | I | insomnia | sleepy/euphoric |
| C4 | C4 Hash | S | anxiety | potent/productive |
| Cab | Caboose | I | insomnia | potent/narcotic |
| CD | California Dream | I | insomnia | narcotic/trippy |
| CO | California Orange | H | anxiety | mild/relaxing |
| Cnk | Cannabisco Kush | H | insomnia | narcotic/trails |
| Cn | Cannadential | H | anxiety | happy/giggly |
| Cah | Cannalope Haze | S | insomnia | up/creative |
| Car | Caramelicious | H | nausea | trippy/happy |
| Crb | Caribbean Dream | H | insomnia | mellow/relaxing |
| Cas | Casey Jones | H | stress | oomph /up/happy |
| Cak | Cataract Kush | H | pain | lazy/happy |
| CH9 | CH9 | S | anxiety | euphoric |
| Chk | Champagne Kush | H | insomnia | up/creative |
| Cw | Charlotte's Web | S | insomnia | exhilarated |
| Che | Cheese | I | pain | trippy/uppity |
| Cb | Chem Berry | H | nausea | calming/relaxing |

| Abr. | Strain | Origin | Med. Use | Effect |
|------|--------|--------|----------|--------|
| Cd | Chemdawg | H | stress | euphoric/creative |
| C4 | Chemdawg 4 | I | pain | trippy/lazy/tired |
| Che | Chernobyl | H | pain | creative/aroused |
| Cak | Cherry Ak-47 | H | anxiety | trippy/uppity/happy |
| Ck | Cherry Kush | H | insomnia | munchies/lazy |
| Chi | Chisel | H | stress | elated |
| Chk | Chocolate Kush | H | pain | creative/chilled |
| Chc | Chocolope | H | stress | uppity/energy |
| Chr | Church OG | I | migraine | trippy/tired |
| Ch | Chronic | H | spasm | mild/euphoric |
| C99 | Cinderella 99 | H | stress | trippy/enhanced |
| Cc | Connie Chung | H | stress | creative/focused |
| Cck | Cotton Candy Kush | I | stress | lethargic /joyful |
| Cj | Cracker Jack | S | stress | energy/refreshed |
| Cbk | Cranberry Kush | I | insomnia | tasty/potent |
| Cc | Cream Caramel | H | insomnia | sedative/heavy |
| DQ | Dairy Queen | H | mood | creative/energy |
| Dv | Darth Vader OG | I | insomnia | tired |
| Dm | Dead Man | H | energy | mild/relaxing |

*Cannabisco Kush*
*A nice new hybrid strain*
*named in honor of*
*cannabis advocate,*
*Paul Cornwell.*

| Abr. | Strain | Origin | Med. Use | Effect |
|------|--------|--------|----------|--------|
| Ds | Death Star | I | stress | tingles/trippy |
| Dep | Deep Purple | I | appetite | lazy/hungry |
| Dia | Diablo | I | insomnia | trippy/tingly |
| Dsl | Diesel | H | anxiety | energy/aromic/A+ |
| Dd | Diesel Duff | H | anxiety | joyful/happy |
| Dsb | DJ Short Blueberry | I | stress | trippy/narcotic |
| D | Doby | H | Anxiety | uplifting/happy |

| Abr. | Strain | Origin | Med. Use | Effect |
|---|---|---|---|---|
| Dom | Domino | I | nausea | lethargic |
| Dnk | Donk | I | appetite | strong/body buzz |
| DD | Double D | I | anxiety | joy/happy |
| Dq | Dream Queen | H | anxiety | up/energy/talkative |
| Dch | Durban Cheese | H | appetite | engrossed |
| Dp | Durban Poison | S | stress | uplifting |
| Dt | Dutch Treat | H | Anxiety | uplifting/euphoric |
| Ed | Ed Rosenthal Super Bud | H | stress | very creative/A+ |
| Ej | El Jeffe | I | migraine | quite trippy |
| Em | El Monstre | H | anxiety | daytime/creative |
| Enl | Endless Sky | I | nausea | potent/mellow |
| Eup | Euphoria | H | pain | trippy/talkative |
| Exo | Exodus Cheese | S | migraines | trippy/ drive |
| Fh | Fire Haze | S | stress | joy/creativity |
| Flo | Flo | H | pain | clear head/intense |
| FL | Free Leonard | H | pain | hashy/potent |
| Fp | Fruity Pebbles | H | anxiety | euphoric/up |
| FMH | Full Melt Hash | H | insomnia | narcotic/potent |
| Fz | Fuzzy Wuzzy | I | insomnia | euphoric/trippy |
| G13 | G-13 | I | stress | trippy |
| 13h | G13 Haze | H | stress | trippy |
| GB | George Bush | H | anxiety | relaxing/giggles |
| Gn | Gnarsly | H | nausea | cerebral/focus |
| Gb | Godberry | I | pain | tingly trip |
| Gdb | God Bud | H | seizures | powerful/clear |
| God | God's Gift | I | pain | lazy/tired |
| Gdg | Golden Goat | H | stress | energetic/creative |
| Gs | Gracie Slick | I | mood | clear/skunky |
| Gh | Grand Hindu | I | spasm | focus |
| Gdp | Granddaddy Purple | I | stress | lazy/tired |
| Ga | Grape Ape | I | pain | lazy/tired/trippy |
| Gcr | Grape Crush | I | migraines | trippy/lazy/joyful |
| Gg | Grape God | H | pain | trippy/euphoric |
| Gks | Grape Kush | H | stress | tired/trippy |
| Gsk | Grape Skunk | I | stress | trippy/lazy |
| Grf | Grapefruit | S | stress | trippy/uppity/tasty |
| Ghz | Grapefruit Haze | H | anxiety | creative/tasty |
| Gk | Grapefruit Kush | H | pain | happy trip/pungent |
| Gvt | Gravity | I | pain | euphoric |

| Abr. | Strain | Origin | Med. Use | Effect |
|------|--------|--------|----------|--------|
| GW | Great White | H | energy | uplifting/motivated |
| GWs | Great White Shark | H | energy | uplifting/happy |
| Gca | Green Candy | S | stress | content /energy |
| Gc | Green Crack | S | stress | energy/euphoric/up |
| Gce | Green Crack Extreme | S | stress | up/talkative/trippy |
| Gdk | Green Door Kush | H | nausea | trippy |
| Gd | Green Dream | H | anxiety | up/energy |
| Gbl | Green Goblin | S | insomnia | trippy/ sedative |
| Gk | Green Kush | I | pain | creative/trippy |
| Go | Green-O-Matic | H | mood | happy/calming |
| Gq | Green Queen | H | insomnia | sleepy/trippy |
| Gk | Guido Kush | I | stress | laid back/lazy |
| Har | Harlequin | H | pain | trippy/uppity |
| Hd | Hash Dog | H | insomnia | strong body buzz |
| Hp | Hash Plant | I | pain | narcotic/potent/trip |

*Power Plant*
*A great hybrid*
*exclusively from*
*Sensi- Seed*
*Company*

| Abr. | Strain | Origin | Med. Use | Effect |
|------|--------|--------|----------|--------|
| Hz | Hashplant Haze | H | migraines | happy days |
| Hg | Hawaii Gold | H | stress | euphoric/happy |
| Hd | Hawaiian Delight | I | pain | narcotic/trippy |
| Hf | Hawaiian Fire | H | appetite | hungry/tingly |
| Haw | Hawaiian Sativa | S | stress | narcotic/trippy |
| Hsk | Hawaiian Skunk | H | stress | enthusiasm |
| Hs | Hawaiian Snow | S | stress | uplifting/trippy |
| H | Haze | S | stress | trippy |
| Hb | Headband | H | anxiety | creative/trippy |
| Hdf | Heavy Duty Fruity | H | spasm | tingly |

| Abr. | Strain | Origin | Med. Use | Effect |
|------|--------|--------|----------|--------|
| Hem | Hempstar | S | stress | up/energy |
| Hj | Herojuana | I | insomnia | lazy/tired |
| Hig | Himalayan Gold | H | pain | inspired /energetic |
| Hk | Hindu Kush | I | pain | narcotic/potent/s |
| Hsk | Hindu Skunk | H | stress | sedated/trippy |
| Hip | Hippie Crippler | H | migraines | narcotic/potent |
| HOG | Hog | I | pain | potent/tingly |
| Hog | Hog's Breath | I | anxiety | productive/happy |
| Hh | Holland's Hope | I | appetite | trippy |
| Hks | Hong Kong Star | H | insomnia | hashy/strong body |
| Huc | Huckleberry | I | stress | uppity/trippy |
| Hgc | Hydro Green Crack | S | stress | enthusiastic |
| Ice | Ice | H | pain | trippy/uppity |
| Inc | Incrediberry | H | stress | even body/uplifting |
| Ind | Indica | H | stress | heavy/purple |
| Ing | Ingrid | I | appetite | munchies/sleepy |
| Imh | Island Maui Haze | H | pain | creative/creeper |
| Iss | Island Sweet Skunk | H | pain | clear/well rounded |
| Ivh | Ivory Haze | S | stress | relaxing |
| J1 | J1 | H | anxiety | blissful /up/trippy |
| J27 | J-27 | S | anxiety | energetic/focused |
| Jf | Jack Flash | H | anxiety | lazed out/talkative |
| JF | Jack Frost | H | stress | uppity/trippy |
| Jc | Jacks Cleaner | S | appetite | skunky/relaxing |
| Jh | Jack Herer | S | stress | narcotic/up/energy |
| Jk | Jack Kush | H | stress | laidback |
| Jtr | Jack the Ripper | H | stress | energy/talkative |
| Jp | Jamaican Pearl | S | nausea | potent/narcotic/joy |
| JF | Jet Fuel | H | pain | uplifting/calming |
| Jil | Jillybean | H | stress | narcotic/up/happy |
| Jh | Jocks Horror | S | anxiety | energetic/refreshed |
| Jf | Juicy Fruit | H | stress | trippy |
| Jup | Jupiter OG | I | pain | energy/focused |
| Kt | K Train | I | pain | trippy |
| KO | KO Kush | H | appetite | calming/tired |
| Kah | Kahuna | H | insomnia | tired/laidback |
| Km | Kali Mist | S | anxiety | potent/trippy |
| Kan | Kandy Kush | H | appetite | happy camper |
| Key | Key Lime Haze | H | nausea | potent/creative |
| Kh | Khola | H | stress | giggles/energy |

73

| Abr. | Strain | Origin | Med. Use | Effect |
|------|--------|--------|----------|--------|
| KC3 | Killer Chem #3 | S | mood | euphoric/mild |
| Kq | Killer Queen | H | anxiety | creative/top rated |
| Kin | King Kong | H | pain | up/creativity |
| Kin | King Kush | I | pain | potent/euphoric |
| Kng | King Louis | I | insomnia | lazy/tired |
| Kb | King's Bread | S | anxiety | euphoric/top rated |
| Kc | King's Cross | I | pain/spasm | trippy/eurphoric |
| Kk | Kings Kush | I | stress | happy/laidback |
| Kry | Kryptonite | I | stress | laidback |
| KF | Kurple Fantasy | H | pain | body/sedative |
| Ku | Kush | I | asthma | tasty/couch lock |
| Kb | Kush Berry | I | nausea | uppity/trippy |
| KH | Kush Hash | H | insomnia | bubble/narcotic |
| La | LA Confidential | I | stress | trippy/euphoric |
| Laj | LA Jack | H | insomnia | trippy |
| Law | LA Woman | H | stress | blissful/energy |
| Lb | Lamb's Bread | S | stress | irie/creative/aroma |
| LB | Lamb's Breath | S | anxiety | mellow/sweet |
| Lav | Lavender | H | stress | trippy/tired |

## Kurple Fantasy

A new strain with hints of
licorice & Kush fire
exclusively from
our friends at
THE CANNASSEUR

| | | | | |
|------|--------|--------|----------|--------|
| LvH | Lavender Hash | I | stress | potent/happy |
| Lav | Lavender Kush | I | insomnia | tired/tingly |
| LGI | Legends Ult. Indica | I | pain | sweet/potent |
| Lem | Lemon Diesel | H | anxiety | focus/uppity |
| Ld | Lemon Drop | I | stress | joyful/happy |

| Abr. | Strain | Origin | Med. Use | Effect |
|------|--------|--------|----------|--------|
| Leg | Lemon G | S | pain | narcotic/creative |
| Lh | Lemon Haze | S | stress | trippy/narcotic/up |
| Lk | Lemon Kush | H | stress | elevating /trippy |
| Lm | Lemon Mazar | I | pain | heavy/potent |
| Log | Lemon OG | I | migraines | stimulated/trippy |
| Ls | Lemon Sativa | S | stress | alert /happy |
| LS | Lemon Skunk | H | pain | lethargic/creative |
| Lif | Lifesaver | H | anxiety | inspired |
| Lag | Lemon Afghani | I | mood | upbeat/chatty |
| Liq | Liquid Butter | I | appetite | lethargic |
| Lsd | LSD | H | stress | narcotic/very trippy |
| M39 | M-39 | H | stress | lazy/ inspired |
| Mad | Madagascar | I | insomnia | joyful / lethargic |
| Mak | Mako Haze | S | anxiety | active |
| Man | Mandala #1 | H | mood | uplifting/potent |
| Mgo | Mango | I | stress | delighted / elevated |
| Mgo | Mango Kush | H | stress | chatty / cheerful |
| Ml | Maple Leaf Indica | I | pain | inspired /trippy |
| MM | Marilyn Monroe | H | pain | potent/strawberry |
| Mar | Mars OG | I | insomnia | drowsy/ lethargic |
| Mg | Martian Mean Green | H | stress | elated /happy |
| Mbb | Master Bubba | I | stress | motivated /tired |
| Mks | Master Kush | H | stress | exhilarated |
| Mkd | Master Kush Diesel | I | anxiety | calming/antianxiety |
| Mma | Master Mango | H | stress | elevated/ sedative |
| Mau | Maui | S | pain | lethargic |
| Mb | Maui Berry | H | anxiety | artistic / content |
| Mw | Maui Waui | S | stress | elevated /narcotic |
| Mz | Mazar | H | nausea | creative/uplifting |
| Mgm | Mean Green Martian | H | anti-inflammatory | uplifting |
| Mp | Mendocino Purps | H | stress/appetite | munchies |
| Mog | Mercury OG | I | stress | euphoric |
| Ms | Mexican Sativa | H | anxiety | exhilarated / peppy |
| Msk | Misty Kush | I | pain | trippy/ blissful |
| Mk | MK Ultra | I | insomnia | idle /happy |
| MD | Moby Dick | S | anxiety | sweet/head high |
| Mo | Moolah | H | mood | pleasing/content |
| Ms | Morning Star | H | anxiety | jubilant / upbeat |

75

| Abr. | Strain | Origin | Med. Use | Effect |
|---|---|---|---|---|
| Mr /relaxed | Mr. Nice | H | stress | exhilarated |
| MrN | Mr. Nice Guy | S | pain | mild/relaxing |
| Neb | Nebula | H | stress | elevated/ inspired |
| Nk | Neptune Kush | I | pain/PMS | exhilarated |
| Nog | Neptune OG | I | stress | elevated/ attentive |
| Nhz | Neville's Haze | H | pain | trippy |
| NbD | New Blue Diesel | H | anxiety | calming/relaxing |
| NT | Night Train | H | insomnia | body/relaxing |
| Nj | Ninja Turtle | H | pain | intense/head high |
| Nl | Northern Lights | I | stress | narcotic |
| N5 | Northern Lights #5 | H | stress | inspired / enriched |
| N7 | Northern Lights #7 | I | pain | heavy/body high |
| Ns | Northern Lights x Skunk | H | pain | clear minded/floaty |
| Nyc | NYC Diesel | H | anxiety | Heavenly / I♥NY |
| NYk | NY Kush | I | mood | active/focused |
| NYs | NYC Sour Diesel | S | anxiety | euphoric/energy |

## Strawberry Diesel

*A blend of Strawberry Cough
and Sour Diesel strains,
predominantly Sativa and a
very potent med from
Reservoir Seeds.*

| | | | | |
|---|---|---|---|---|
| Ody | Odyssey | H | anxiety | jubilant /uplifted |
| Ogh | OG Headband | H | anxiety | sweet/potent |
| Og | OG Kush | H | stress | lethargic /narcotic |
| Ogp | OG Poison | H | insomnia | languid |

| Abr. | Strain | Origin | Med. Use | Effect |
|------|--------|--------|----------|--------|
| Ogw | OG Wreck | H | nausea | narcotic/trippy |
| OGi | OGiesel | H | anxiety | jovial |
| Orb | Orange Bud | I | anxiety | engrossed |
| Oc | Orange Crush | H | stress | happy |
| Od | Orange Dream | H | stress | happy |
| Ok | Orange Kush | H | insomnia | drowsy |
| Ov | Orange Velvet | H | migraines | lethargic / absorbed |
| Ord | Organic Diesel | H | appetite | sedative /euphoric |
| OM | Original Misty | H | seizures | potent/narcotic |
| Pan | Panama Red | S | pain | peppy / elevated |
| Pap | Papaya | H | migraines | lifted /euphoric |
| Per | Permafrost | H | stress | creative |
| Prp | Perplex | I | insomnia | body high/tired |
| Pin | Pineapple | H | pain | lethargic |
| Pd | Pineapple Diesel | H | anxiety | trippy/ stimulating |
| Pex | Pineapple Express | H | stress | contentment / bliss |
| Pk | Pineapple Kush | H | pain/appetite | hungry/ listless |
| Pit | Pineapple Thai | I | stress | lethargic/ euphoric |
| Ptw | Pineapple Trainwreck | S | appetite | narcotic/spacey |
| PK | Platinum Kush | I | stress | lethargic |
| Plt | Platinum OG | I | anxiety | exhilarated |
| Ppk | Platinum Purple Kush | I | insomnia | blissful / lethargic |
| Plm | Plum | H | insomnia | body & head buzz |
| Plu | Pluto Kush | I | pain | peppy / drowsy |
| Phz | Poison Haze | S | appetite | enthusiastic |
| Pog | Pot of Gold | I | pain | lethargic /hungry |
| Pow | Power Plant | I | stress | chatty/ inspired |
| Pn | Pure Afghan | I | pain | narcotic/trippy |
| PG | Pure Gold | H | insomnia | relaxed/lazy |
| Pur | Pure Kush | I | insomnia | sleepy/ lethargic |
| Pp | Pure Power | I | pain | lethargic/productive |
| Pa | Purple Afghani | I | insomnia | sleepy/lazy |
| Pb | Purple Buddha | I | pain | laziness/ silly |
| PB | Purple Butter | I | pain | strong body buzz |
| Pc | Purple Candy | I | pain | inspired /tingly/lazy |
| Pc | Purple Cream | I | stress | blissful |
| Pd | Purple Diesel | S | stress | trippy/narcotic |
| PE | Purple Erkle | H | anxiety | head&body/subtle |
| Pg | Purple Goo | I | anxiety | lifted /euphoric |

| Abr. | Strain | Origin | Med. Use | Effect |
|------|--------|--------|----------|--------|
| Php | Purple Hashplant | H | insomnia | lethargic |
| Ph | Purple Haze | S | stress | trippy/ inspired |
| Ppk | Purple Kush | I | stress | lethargic / drowsy |
| Pmn | Purple Mr. Nice | I | insomnia | lethargic |
| Pn | Purple Nepal | I | anxiety | heavy high/night |
| Pp | Purple Passion | I | appetite | munchies |
| Pp | Purple Princess | H | stress | lethargic |
| Psd | Purple Sour Diesel | H | stress | elevated /energetic |
| Pt | Purple Tonic | I | insomnia | sleepy/ sedative |
| PT | Purple Trainwreck | H | stress | trippy/narcotic |
| Pu | Purple Urkle | I | insomnia | lethargic /lazy |
| Pwr | Purple Wreck | I | pain | elated /munchies |
| Que | Querkle | H | stress | tingly/ elevating |
| Rsk | Raspberry Kush | I | anxiety | trippy |
| Rec | Recon | H | anxiety | creative/focused |
| Red | Red Dragon | H | anxiety | delighted |
| Rd | Red Dwarf | I | migraines | lethargic |
| Rhz | Red Haze | S | migraine | narcotic/energy |
| Rr | Richie Rich | H | anxiety | narcotic/trippy |
| Rg | Romping Goddess | H | anxiety | jovial |
| Rom | Romulan | I | stress | lethargic |
| Rg | Romulan Grapefruit | H | stress | narcotic/tasty |
| Rbk | Root Beer Kush | S | nausea | productive |
| Rrf | Russian Rocket Fuel | H | nausea | enthusiastic /trippy |
| Sd | Sadhu | I | pain | hashy/creative |
| Sg | Sage | H | stress | elevating/ inspiring |
| Sns | Sage N Sour | S | anxiety | trippy/ inspired |
| SJ | Sannie Jack | H | seizures | potent/Herer hybrid |
| Sat | Satori | H | insomnia | trippy/tingly |
| Sb | Seattle Blue | I | migraines | driven /euphoric |
| Sen | Sensi Star | I | pain | lethargic |
| SAK | Sensi Star x AK-47 | H | pain | couch lock/narcotic |
| SvH | Sevendust Haze | H | insomnia | narcotic/smooth |
| Shm | Shaman | S | anxiety | productive |
| Shk | Shark Shock | I | appetite | munchies/tingly |
| Shp | Shipwreck | S | pain | trippy/euphoric |
| Shi | Shishkaberry | H | anxiety | elevating / silly |
| Sh | Shiva Skunk | H | stress | blissful |
| Sln | Shoreline | H | anxiety | narcotic/euphoric |
| Slv | Silver Haze | H | stress | productive high |

| Abr. | Strain | Origin | Med. Use | Effect |
|------|--------|--------|----------|--------|
| Svp | Silver Pearl | H | anxiety | blissful /happy |
| Sil | Silver Surfer | H | insomnia | sleepy/ lethargic |
| SvT | Silver Tip | H | stress | euphoric/top shelf |
| Sig | Silverback Gorilla | I | pain | lethargic |
| Sk1 | Skunk #1 | S | stress | euphoric/ peppy |
| S11 | Skunk #11 | H | anxiety | creeper/euphoric |
| Skd | Skunky Diesel | H | pain | uplifting/ blissful |
| Sky | Skywalker | H | insomnia/stress | tired/lazy |
| SOK | Skywalker OG Kush | H | insomnia | narcotic/strong |
| Sno | Snowcap | S | anxiety | trippy/happy |
| Sou | Soul Shine | H | stress | narcotic/trippy |
| Sa | Sour Apple | H | insomnia | idle /tingly/nice |
| Sch | Sour Chocolate | S | insomnia | drowsy |
| Sd | Sour Diesel | S | stress | trippy/uppity/ bliss |
| Sdr | Sour Dream | H | stress | euphoric/joyful |
| Sf | Sour Flower | S | pain | drive / elevating |
| Sg | Sour Grapes | H | stress | elated / lifted |
| Sk | Sour Kush | H | migraine | absorbed / lethargic |
| Sog | Sour OG | H | stress | euphoric/ elevated |
| Sk | Space Kush | H | headache | mild body/numbing |
| Sqk | Space Queen | H | stress | elated / blissful |
| Sp | Spurkle | I | anxiety | relaxed |
| Spt | Sputnix | H | pain | euphoric/smooth |
| SN | Star Nebula | I | anxiety | very potent/night |
| Sc | Strawberry Cough | H | stress | lifted /trippy/happy |
| ScH | Strawberry Cough Hash | H | pain | narcotic/productive |
| SD | Strawberry Diesel | H | pain/nausea | tasty/potent |
| Sk | Strawberry Kush | I | anxiety | trippy/ sedative |
| Sp | Stinky Pete | S | anxiety | energy/uplifting |
| SGS | Sugar Green Skunk | H | pain | couch lock/creeper |
| SS | Sugar Skunk | H | anxiety | clear headed/active |
| Shk | Sugar Shack | H | pain | uplifting/euphoric |
| Sbd | Super Blue Dream | H | pain | lethargic |
| Sgc | Super Green Crack | S | stress | active/ spirited |
| Slh | Super Lemon Haze | H | stress | uplifted/ active |
| Ss | Super Silver Haze | S | stress | narcotic/ inspired |
| Ssk | Super Skunk | H | stress | content / bliss |
| Ssd | Super Sour Diesel | S | stress | productive / jovial |
| Sup | Superman OG | I | insomnia | lethargic /munchies |
| Sd | Sweet Diesel | S | anxiety | productive / silly |

| Abr. | Strain | Origin | Med. Use | Effect |
|------|--------|--------|----------|--------|
| SD | Sweet Dreams | I | anxiety | strong/creeper |
| Sis | Sweet Island Skunk | H | anxiety | elevating /euphoric |
| Swe | Sweet Kush | H | pain | inspired /uppity |
| St | Sweet Tooth | H | anxiety | lethargic |
| St3 | Sweet Tooth #3 | H | pain | sweet/sedative |
| Swb | Swiss Bliss | H | pain | tingly/ chatty |
| Tog | Tahoe OG | I | nausea | narcotic/ lethargic |
| Tan | Tangerine Kush | I | stress | peppy / elevated |
| Twv | Thaidal Wave | H | anxiety | trippy/euphoric |
| Tt | Thai-Tanic | H | nausea | exhilarated / chatty |
| Thc | THC bomb | H | PMS/pain | robust / content |
| TB | The Black | H | pain/nausea | narcotic |
| TC | The Church | H | mood | giggly/euphoric |
| Tfl | The Flav | H | stress | potent/narcotic |
| Tp | The Purp | I | anxiety | euphoric/productive |
| Tig | Tiger Woods | H | stress | blissful / elated |
| Tw | Trainwreck | H | stress | trippy/uplifting |
| Trt | Tropical Tang | H | appetite | content /munchies |
| Tc | Tropicali | H | migraine | trippy/narcotic |
| TI | Twilight Indica | I | anxiety | 100% Afghan/ glad |
| UK | UK Cheese | H | stress | euphoric/joyful |
| UAk | Ultimate Afghan Kush | I | pain | mildly psychedelic |
| Utw | Ultimate Trainwreck | S | anxiety | narcotic/euphoric |
| Van | Vanilla Kush | I | pain | lazy/tingly |
| Vog | Venice OG | S | stress | chatty/ blissful |
| Vbh | Very Berry Haze | S | pain | peppy / absorbed |
| Vdo | Voodoo | S | pain | trippy/narcotic |
| VOR | Vortex | H | asthma | motivated/active |
| Wa | Waldo | H | anxiety | creative/euphoric |
| WaK | Walrus Kush | H | appetite | content / silly |
| WA | Wappa | H | stress | potent/stoney |
| War | Warlock | H | stress | trippy/creative |
| Wb | White Berry | H | stress | creative/trippy |
| WH | White Haze | I | anxiety | clear/eurphoric |
| WI | White Ice | H | anxiety | tired/nighttime |
| Wq | White Queen | H | migraine | narcotic/euphoric |
| Wr | White Rhino | H | stress | lethargic /euphoric |
| Wr | White Russian | H | stress | narcotic/ inspired |
| Whi | White Shark | S | stress | cheerful /creative |

| Abr. | Strain | Origin | Med. Use | Effect |
|------|--------|--------|----------|--------|
| Ww | White Widow | H | stress | stoney/narcotic |
| Wz | White Zombie | H | stress | productive / elated |
| Ww | Wonder Woman | H | appetite | hunger/energy |
| Ww | Wonderwoman OG | I | anxiety | trippy/ lethargic |
| X13 | XJ-13 | H | stress | narcotic/ inspiring |
| Yod | Yoda OG | I | stress | trippy/ content |

*Source for abbreviations, www.leafly.com

# Types of cannabis concentrates
## HASHISH " HASH"

Hashish is a common concentrate whose use dates back to ancient times. It is comprised of a collection of marijuana's resinous glands or trichomes which is gentle heated and with applied pressure the gland's heads break, releasing a viscous liquid. The pressure has forced all the air from the glands leaving a mass of crushed glands which are compacted into cakes, slabs, or rolled into balls. There are basic methods for collecting these resinous glands, mostly sifting and hand rubbing.

Hand rubbing hash is collected right from the plant while the resin is still sticky. While the yield is often low, the quality of hash can be exceptional high. Hand rubbed hash usually comes in a ball. Hash ranges in colors, most typically a blond or a black tar color. Pliability also varies from the different types of hash and processes.

A chunk of hashish

Before the decriminalization of medical marijuana, hashish was quite rare and hard to come by.  After the heightened security after 9/11, most all hash you will encounter is produced and manufactured in the US.  Countries like Turkey, India, Afghanistan, Pakistan and Lebanon were all producers of hashish showing up in the US pre 9/11.

The hash now being produced in medical marijuana states will challenge even the finest hash from these other countries.

High quality hash should soften from the warmth of your hands.

There are typically four types of hash; water hash, finger hash(hand rubbed), bubble and sieve.

Legend has it that Afghani farmers would run through their cannabis fields in a suit of leather then scrape finger hash off with their knives.

Water hash historically is made by putting cannabis in a jug with ice and water and then vigorously shaking it.  THC crystals clump together and in a cold environment with the ice the crystals sink.  The crystals are then collected and used to process into hash.

Sieve hash is collected by shaking the buds of the plant over a screen and collecting the crystals that fall through.  What is collected is kief.  The kief crystals must be heated  and pressed going through a chemical change when heated and then processed into hash.

Bubble hash is the majority of what is on the market today in Colorado dispensaries.  Bubble hash is the result of a combination of water hash and sieve hash.  The cold water and ice produce the crystals which float to the bottom and nylon filters separate the crystals into various layers.

Hash can be ingested orally, or most frequently is smoked in a smaller pipe, referred to as a "hash pipe" or under glass.

The method used to smoke hash under glass is to take a piece of cardboard and stick a pin through the bottom.  Place the piece of hash on the pin and light it.  The hash itself will slowly ignite.  Once it does, blow out the flame, the hash will now smolder.  Now, place a glass over the top capturing all the smoke.  To take a hit simply put your mouth to the edge of the glass, lightly lift it and suck in the smoke.

## KIEF

Kief is a powder made up of loose glands shaken from marijuana buds.  It resembles sand in appearance.  In Holland you will hear this referred to as "pollen" which might help explain kief.

Kief can be smoked as it is or added to a joint or bowl with bud marijuana. It can also be pressed to make hash. This is one of the easiest and cheapest ways to make hash at home.

Kief

Kief is sometimes used for tinctures and cooking as some people express that cooking with cannabis leaf gives food an unpleasant strong green flavor.

## HASH OIL

Hash oil is an evaporated solution of tetrahydrocannabinol and various other compounds produced by a solvent extraction of cannabis. Despite the similarity in names, it does not resemble hashish. It can be a very potent medication due to its high THC concentration, which generally varies between 70 - 90 percent.

Related Honey oil is a specific type of hash oil produced by certain solvents, most commonly butane, and isopropanol. Both hash and honey oil is traditionally a dark, viscous liquid made by solvent extraction of cannabis resin.

Hash Oil is black in appearance and usually
Packaged in gram vials.

Hash oil can be consumed in various ways. It can be Smeared on
a joint or added to the inner rim of a pipe bowl.
Mixed in food or may be vaporized. For years oil has been
traditionally smoked in an 'oil pipe". A glass pipe which consists
of a glass stem and an end that resembles a glass bubble with a
small hole, the oil is applied to the inside of the glass bubble
using a pin or similar device. A flame is then held under the
bubble vaporizing the oils in the bubble which is inhaled through
the stem.

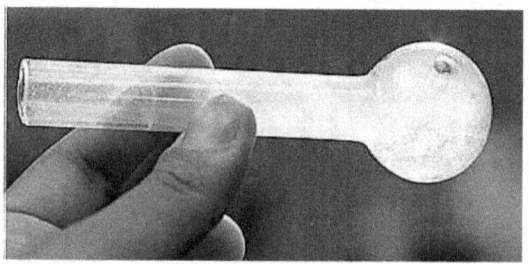

An "oil" pipe used to smoke hash oil

Hash oil none the less produces a very potent narcotic like high,
and care should be exercised to take it slow to find the correct
dosage that works for you. Hash oil is an excellent sleep aid for
those patients suffering from insomnia.

## RICK SIMPSON OIL

For several years I had been occasionally hearing about this "miracle oil" made by a Canadian named Rick Simpson. This oil was a hemp based oil and was reported to have extreme medicinal value. It was reported not to have that psychoactive effect or "high" associated with THC.

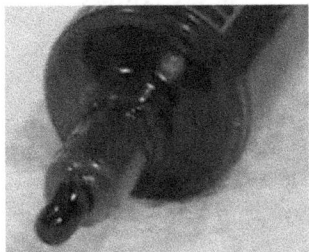

The miracle "Simpson Oil"

In 2002, Simpson discovered medical qualities in a hemp oil he had developed. Simpson discovered that his oil could cure cancer and the majority of serious diseases. He produced this oil and distributed it for free to people who could benefit from it. Of course, he ended up arrested several times for doing this. He now lives in Europe to avoid charges for what will be his third arrest for manufacturing and trafficking.

However let's look at the facts, there is now just too much evidence and too many testimonials to support Simpson's claim. Over the past seven years, seventy percent of the patients who maintained Simpson's regiment for treatment were totally cancer free after a treatment consisting of ingesting a total of sixty grams.

People who use Simpson oil utilize doses of either one third gram, three times daily or one half gram, twice daily. Simpson oil users report to be relaxed and sleepy after about an hour following dosing.

There are many imitators out there; however Simpson publically posts his recipe for his oil. It usually comes in a syringe and users squeeze out doses .

I strongly suggest that all patients take a serious look and do research about the amazing healing properties of this product. For this truly may qualify for some as a miracle cure for some ailments for those who can access to true Simpson oil.

# Effects of Cannabis at temperature

| °F | | Effects on Marijuana |
|---|---|---|
| 68°-75° | normal | The most volatile terpenes gradually Vaporize, producing marijuana's Tell tale smell |
| 212° | boiling water | THC-acid is completely decarboxylated after 90 minutes |
| 265°-300° | low temp vaporizer | the most volatile terpenes will vaporize altogether. THC-acid will gradually decarboxlate,very little THC vaporizes |
| 300° | oven | 5 minutes kills all aspergillus fungus spores and destroys dangerous pathogens |
| 355°-400° | ideal vaporizer | terpenes completely vaporize and 5%-10% of THC vaporizes in approx. 90 seconds |
| 445° | hot vaporizer | THC completely decarboxylates in approx. 5 minutes and approx. 30% of THC vaporizes in 30 seconds |
| 455° | flame | Marijuana ignites and terpenes and THC are released in the smoke |

*Source: Marijuana Medical Handbook, Gieringer, Rosenthal, Carter & personal notes*

# COMING TO COLORADO
## IN 2014-2015

# DENNIS PERON & MICHAEL MALOTT
## Book signing and Lecture Tour
## The Father of Medical Marijuana &
## The Author of the
## Colorado Medical Marijuana
## Handbook & Connsieurs
## Handbook Together

## COMING TO A CITY NEAR YOU

Dennis Peron is a legendary figure within the medical marijuana industry. Known as the "father of medical marijuana", Dennis almost singlehandedly legalized medical marijuana in California and introduced medical marijuana to this country. He also opened the San Francisco Cannabis Buyers Club, the very first medical marijuana dispensary in U.S. history.

Michael Malott is a former Peron employee from the mid 90's who worked at Peron's dispensary and for Peron when he drafted the Compassionate Use Act. Malott continues to work in the industry and has written and published six medical marijuana specific titles including Peron's authorized biography and the Colorado Medical Marijuana Handbook.

## Contaminates

One of the dangers of both smoking and eating marijuana is the potential contamination of bacteria or fungus spores, like Aspergillus which can result in a serious even life threatening risk to AIDS patients. Therefore, cannabis users susceptible to these threats are best advised to sterilize the marijuana they intend to smoke. Contamination is not highly common, but there have been reports of patients getting Aspergillosis, a lung infection caused by the inhalation of aspergillus fungus spores. This is particularly dangerous, even deadly to HIV patients.

According to expert, Ed Rosenthal marijuana should be dried to a 10%-15% water content in order to prevent the growth of fungus.

A common question is why these dangerous pathogens aren't killed during smoking? Smoke also passes through a cooler, unburned material when inhaled and pathogens can enter the smoke stream and infect the patient.

Although the risk of infection may be minimal, patients suffering from a weaker immune system are recommended to sterilize their marijuana prior to consuming.

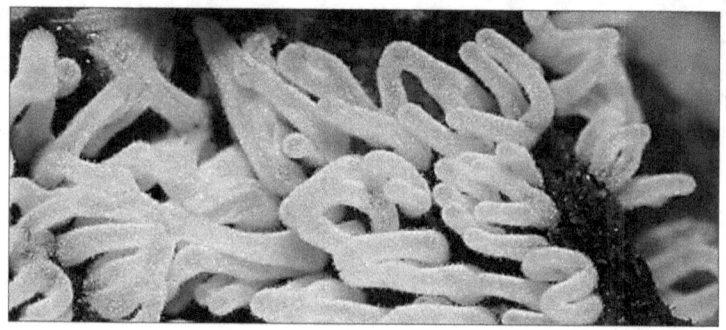
Mold spores on cannabis

Uncontaminated marijuana produces a minty or aromatic odor. Once infested, the smell changes to a stale and musty odor. Contaminated marijuana which is undergoing rapid decay may even feel warm to the touch.

*"demonstrated that spores of Aspergillus fumigatus and Mucor species survive in smoke drawn from marijuana cigarettes. Also, some microbiological toxins are not degraded by combustion"*
*Kurup,V.P., A. Resnick, S.L. Kagen, S. H. Cohen and J. N. Fink. 1983. Allergenic fungi and actinomycetes in smoking materials and their health implications. Mycopathologia*

Cannabis which is contaminated with mold is completely unusable. Mold in some cases may not even be visible to the naked eye. Avoid marijuana that has any kind of a moldy smell, or otherwise alerts your suspicions.

Molds commonly associated with marijuana include; Rhizopus nigrans, Mucor hiemalis, Penicillin chrysogenum, P. italicum, Aspergillus flavus, A. fumigatus, A. niger.

Carefully cultivated and harvested marijuana harbors a minimum threat of containing hazardous microorganisms. For added protection, material must be screened for contamination before it is packaged for use as medical marijuana. Since opportunistic infections pose the greatest danger to immunosuppressed patients, marijuana should be sterilized.

Lastly, patients must be given careful instructions to ensure their marijuana does not become contaminated prior to use.

The best protection is lab testing which is being done in several states. The below is an example of a lab report from Traverse City, Michigan based Herbal Elements which includes THC, CBD, and CBN level reports.

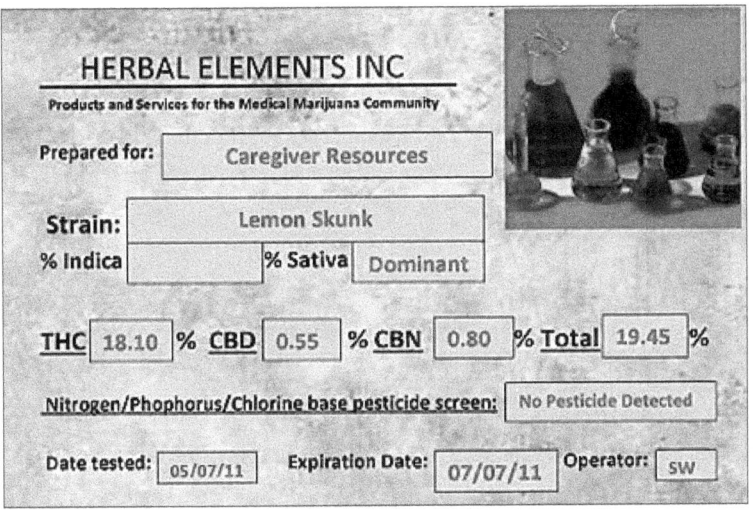

Sample of a typical Lab Test Card issued by Herbal Elements

Some may remember the highly controversial Paraquat contamination of Mexican Sativa during late seventies which was financed by the US Government. Paraquat is a commonly used pesticide which is labeled as being toxic to humans. It was later concluded that the contamination of Cannabis coming into the US, did no toxic harm to users. Others have linked it to the development of Parkinson's Disease.

## Sterilizing Marijuana

Sterilization is an important process for HIV & AIDS patients as well as some patients who suffer from an illness which make them highly susceptible to contaminates.

Back at Harborside in Oakland, California medical marijuana is tested upon acquisition to ensure the cannabis is entirely free of any mold, insecticides or other pathogens which could prove harmful to those with frail immune systems. This is similar to what Steve Webber is doing up in Traverse City with his company, Herbal Elements.

In the Netherlands, cannabis is treated with gamma radiation to eliminate all pathogens and ensure it is acceptable for consumption.

Fret not, effective sterilization is relatively simple and can be accomplished with only the oven.

Medical marijuana can be sterilized by simply placing the marijuana into your oven at a temperature of 300° F for five minutes. Preheat the oven and simply place the marijuana on a baking sheet. Do not use aluminum foil as it emits ions when heated.

Be careful not to overheat as THC vaporizes at higher temperatures and marijuana becomes extremely brittle with any less than 10% water content.

Once your marijuana is serialized, you can even mist it lightly with a water bottle and store in a container or baggie to ensure it does not become too brittle.

# Medical uses for marijuana

Marijuana has been in use since the earliest documented times for medical purposes and treatment. The United States government does not recognize this. As more and more people benefit from the use of cannabis, and more states, major medical organizations, and such continue to recognize this fact, the government will have no choice but to accept the facts.


*"All use of marijuana is medical"*
**Dennis Peron**


## Adolescent Treatment - ADHD, ADD

Medical marijuana and children? That rubs a lot of people the wrong way and brings up a highly controversial topic, but the truth is medical marijuana has saved children's lives period. Case in point, two-year-old Cash Hyde, Montana's youngest medical marijuana patient. Cash was diagnosed with a brain tumor at age one. Doctors tried several medications and his father sat beside him in the hospital for forty days while Cash didn't eat and his heart stopped on one occasion. Cash's dad then elected to try medical marijuana and today Cash is home living the life a child should be living, playing, running and enjoying life. His brain tumor, in complete remission.

Look at the medications doctors are prescribing to children now. Medicines to control ADHD, ADD, hyperactivity, and more. These medications are stimulants like amphetamines, Ritalin, etc. These psychoactive drugs are in reality far more dangerous than medical marijuana to a child. Medical marijuana has been stereotyped for so long that it's hard for people to understand that medical marijuana can be a tremendous asset to treating children. I have personally witnessed in California where children have had tremendous benefit from the use of medical marijuana prescribed by their pediatrician for certain ailments and disorders.

Recently, the head of the Autism Research Institute of America called medical marijuana "a miracle treatment for Autism". I have seen a child who was diagnosed with Autism treated with medical marijuana and after one and a half years of receiving a medical marijuana tincture, doctors were no longer able to even diagnose that child had Autism. The medical marijuana had allowed certain receptors to slow down and it allowed the child to focus. That child is currently enrolled in a public school with other children his own age and nobody even knows he once had Autism. In this case, medical marijuana allowed a then three-year-old child to completely overcome Autism with a year and a half of treatment with medical marijuana, the only drug the child was taking. I can't argue those facts, because that child was my very own son, Zachary and I personally witnessed my child's complete treatment.

On the website of Donald C Clark MD & Associates is a story of a Colorado mom, who is also a teacher at the local high school who treated her 13-year-old son with medical marijuana with exceptional success and of others who have also found cannabis to be an exceptional tool to battle Autism.  So, as time goes by and cannabis becomes more accepted as a drug with phenomenal medical potential, I believe you will see it commonly prescribed to children who suffer from ADHD, ADD, Autism, and other disorders.

I wholehearted recommend that any parent looking for a breakthrough with an Autistic child, look into the option of treating that child with medical marijuana.  Its results are mindboggling.  In the case I personally witnessed it changed a withdrawn Autistic child into a normal functioning child who you could never tell once had Autism in a little more than one year of treatment.  That child ceased taking cannabis after a year and a half and no longer requires medical marijuana.

In 2004, a brilliant doctor from Ventura, California by the name of Claudia Jensen gave Congressional testimony before the U.S. House Government Reform Subcommittee; she knew the benefits of treating adolescents with medical marijuana and had found that cannabis was uniquely beneficial in treatment for some children.

Likewise, treatment of children suffering from ADHD, and ADD with medical cannabis looks quite promising.

There are several other documented cases clearly showing the benefits of some childhood disorders being best treated with medical marijuana and in fact, the news program 20/20 recently featured cases of children being treated with medical marijuana and endorsed those efforts.

## AIDS & HIV

The standard medications used to currently treat HIV patients have been known to cause severe nausea. With medical breakthroughs and advancements and the introduction of inhibitors which can now prolong a patient's life indefinitely, treatment requires a regime of prescription drugs that can be quite overwhelming and nauseating. Some HIV patients suffer from severe appetite and weight loss commonly known as "wasting syndrome" a condition that is serious and which can be absolutely life threatening. AIDS patients and their doctors have found that medical marijuana effectively helps fight the nausea, stimulate appetite and maintain their regime with such amazing results that patients who start using medical marijuana have reported weight gains of up to 50 pounds in just weeks.

One study done by the Stanford School of Medicine, found that HIV medical marijuana users were 3.3 times likely to adhere to their anti-retroviral therapy.

A 2003 study published by the University of California at San Francisco showed a 20% increase in T cell counts by medical marijuana users.

Marijuana has certainly now gained wide spread acceptance by AIDS patients and doctors across the world as a highly effective and worthwhile treatment.

Patients should sterilize their marijuana before smoking or ingesting to eliminate any existing bacteria or fungus spores *(See sterilization).* Aspergillis spores can cause a life-threatening lung disease in AIDS patients and is still highly toxic even to healthy individuals.

Medical marijuana treatment has not shown to have any negative effects for AIDS patients or to have any negative impact on the immune system.

## Alzheimer's disease

AD or as it is also commonly known, senile dementia is classified as a progressive degenerative disorder. It is characterized by its progressive deterioration of overall cognitive functioning, this including lapses in memory.

Behavior patterns of an AD patient can include loss of appetite, agitation and aggressive behavior and depression. Alzheimer's attacks by the formation of plaques in the brain. There are few drugs out to relieve the symptoms of

AD, and their long term outcome is not very favorable. AD becomes fatal when it causes too great an amount of brain damage.

A recent study at the Scripps Research Institute made an amazing discovery that THC could actually retard the progression of AD. Researchers concluded that THC was considerably superior to FDA drugs used to treat AD and might help treat both the symptoms and progression of AD.

The British Journal of Pharmacology has concluded that *"Cannabinoids offer a multi-faceted approach for the treatment of Alzheimer's disease by providing neuroprotection and reducing neuroinflammation, whilst simultaneously supporting the brains intrinsic repair mechanisms"*.

## Analgesia

Thousands of years ago, people used cannabis as an analgesia to prepare patients for surgery and for pain relief. Cannabis has been used to provide relief almost as far back as we can date. Since those times marijuana has been used for treatment of a vast number of ailments, from PMS to severe chronic pain.

## Anti-nausea / appetite stimulant

Cannabis has been consistently found to treat and suppress nausea and motivate appetite since its introduction to modern medicine in the early nineteenth century. It is nothing short of a miracle treatment for the side effects of cancer treatment which uses high level radiation and chemotherapy. The impact on the body is intensely severe. It is expected that patients will experience severe nausea and vomiting following treatment, even lasting for days. Many medications have been used to help a patient cope with this horrifying ordeal and get through treatment. Even so, the stress and treatment is so severe that many patients simply choose not to undergo chemotherapy and simply give in to the natural progression of the disease.

During the 1980's several states sponsored clinical studies of medical marijuana to treat cancer patients. Patients in these states reported medical marijuana to be an effective anti-nauseant, some states reporting success in over 90% of the patients studied.

The drugs commonly prescribed by doctors to treat these treatment side effects are in most cases, ineffective in providing relief to these patients. Most notable of these was a drug called, Marinol which was approved by the FDA in 1986 for use with cancer patients. Studies began surfacing that showed that patients who smoked marijuana had such far greater and faster results in dealing with the side effects of chemotherapy than those who were using pharmaceutical drugs prescribed by their doctor's. Doctor's under the protection of the First Amendment began recommending medical marijuana to their patients undergoing chemotherapy.

Musician Melissa Etheridge was one celebrity who was launched into the medical marijuana spotlight after being diagnosed with cancer and then openly raved about how marijuana helped her get through her rigorous treatment. Every one of her doctors recommended that she use medical marijuana.

In a Harvard University survey of oncologists, nearly half reported they would prescribe cannabis if they were able to do so.

## Anti-convulsant and anti-spasmodic

It is documented that cannabis has been used to treat epilepsy back in medieval times.

Cannabinoids have certain anticonvulsant properties and have been reported to help manage and control muscle spasms.

Cannabis is useful for a number of spasm-inducing disorders, including multiple sclerosis, spinal injuries and other conditions and patients have frequently reported that they are able to eliminate or reduce their intake of prescription drugs and better control their symptoms with medical marijuana.

## Anti-inflammation

Many arthritis patients have reported that cannabis use reduces pain and inflammation. Cannabis has very unique anti-inflammatory properties. THC has the ability to inhibit the aggregation of the immune system's platelet cells, which is the principal cause of inflammation.

## Anxiety

Anxiety is commonly treated with drugs like Valium or Librium, which are benzodiazepines. Some patients prefer using cannabis to benzodiazepines. It is possible that Cannabis can aggravate anxiety and trigger panic attacks, especially in inexperienced users. These panic attacks can be anything from a heightened paranoia to severe paranoia and panic. We all know a story about, or experienced firsthand someone smoking cannabis and their anxiety level got so high that the person got scared and sought emergency medical treatment. Seasoned cannabis smokers appear to be less prone to panic attacks or anxiety.

## Arthritis

Unquestionable cannabis has benefits for people who suffer from Arthritis and Rheumatism and has a long history of use for such. Patients have reported that cannabis use has successfully worked as an antispasmodic and anti-inflammatory agent and has worked to relieve pain associated with these disorders. Many patients have found the greatest benefit of cannabis in treating the chronic pain of severe arthritis or rheumatism of the joints. Cannabis works to also relieve the painful muscle spasms that are often associated with Rheumatism.

Fibromyalgia patients have also reported great success with use of cannabis. Fibromyalgia is a mysterious rheumatism type disease with widespread musculoskeletal pain like symptoms with tender spots in the back and neck areas. People suffering from fibromyalgia also are prone to fatigue.

A recent study in Germany found oral THC effective in reducing pain by up to two-thirds.

Patients suffering from severe chronic arthritis, rheumatism and fibromyalgia often respond better to larger doses taken orally. Use extreme care in increasing any current dosage.

## Asthma

Asthma is characterized as an allergic condition in which the lining of the lungs become inflamed and swollen and result in causing acute attacks of breathlessness and wheezing. These attacks are commonly treated with bronchodilators which relax and expand air passageways.

Many patients have reported cannabis useful in relieving asthma attacks. It has been found that THC itself acts like a bronchodilator. Studies have consistently found that both smoked and ingested marijuana can relieve asthmatic spasms in patients.

In comparison studies, cannabis was determined to have a milder peak effect, but to overall act longer than bronchodilators.

One concern with patients was smoking marijuana since the smoke creates irritation in some patients. Vaporizers are an excellent alternative for people concerned with this.

## Attention Deficit Hyperactivity Disorder (ADHD)

See adolescent treatment

## Autism

See adolescent treatment

## Autoimmune inflammatory diseases

A good example of how cannabis is effective in treating immune attacks against the nerves cells' protective coating is cannabis's effects on multiple sclerosis patients. Likewise cannabis is effective in treating other inflammatory and autoimmune disorders. Another example is diabetes mellitus, a disease linked to excess insulin due to the bodies inability to produce sufficient insulin. Type 1 diabetes is usually related to autoimmune damage to the pancreas, type 2 is linked to genetics and dietary factors.

Studies have shown that CBD can reduce the incidence of diabetes, lower inflammatory proteins in the blood and help protect against retinal degeneration which leads to blindness.

Patients have also found cannabis effective in treating the pain associated with diabetic neuropathy.

## Cancer

Cancer patients have long benefited from medical marijuana use and we proved that smoking marijuana does not increase our chances of getting cancer. There is increasing evidence to show that cannabinoids have anti-tumoral properties and tests have been done where the direct application of THC and CBD reduce the size of certain cancers. We are now even seeing evidence that cannabinoids attack cancer cells while leaving healty cells untouched. In Madrid, patients with brain tumors and other forms of cancer are successfully being treated with cannabis medications.
Many leading doctors and experts believe that cannabinoids represent a whole new class of effective anti-cancer drugs.

Tests done at Harvard University have proven that THC shrinks lung cancer tumors in size and weight by 50%, and

THC reduces cancer lesions by 60%. Cannabis has reportedly stopped breast cancer from spreading.

There is increasing evidence supporting that various Cannabinoids and endo-cannabinoids can inhibit proliferation of other cancer cell lines, including lung, prostate, breast, colorectal, gastric, pancreatic, leukemia and forms of lymphoma.

*See- Rick Simpson oil for important information*

## Cardiovascular

Smoking medical marijuana is not recommended for people with cardiovascular disorders. Smoking marijuana speeds up the heart by as much as 60 beats per minute, and lasting roughly an hour.

"The smoking of marijuana causes changes in the heart and circulation which are characteristic of stress" as warned by the National Academy of Sciences.

The increase in the work of the heart after smoking marijuana is dangerous for patients with hypertension cerebrovascular disease and coronary atherosclerosis.

Some heart patients report chest pains or other discomfort after smoking marijuana and this can trigger false trips to the emergency room.  THC also may cause a modest increase in blood pressure.

There is documented studies that show that people who continue to smoke marijuana after having a heart attack are at a greater risk then those who abstained from continued marijuana use.  If you desire to continue to smoke marijuana you should consult with your doctor and see about using a beta-blocker drug prescribed by your doctor.

## Cerebral palsy

Cerebral palsy is the result of a central nervous system injury during birth which results in a movement disorder. At the present date there have been no clinical studies of medical marijuana use for the treatment of cerebral palsy, however patients have reported success with cannabis use in controlling muscle spasm.

## Choreas

Choreas is a disorder characterized by uncontrollable complex and jerky movements.  Huntington's choreas, the disorder that claimed folk artist, Woody Guthrie is a progressive, degenerative disease tied back to genetics.

## Chronic Fatigue Syndrome

Patients report that they can treat chronic fatigue syndrome with medical marijuana with successful results. Chronic fatigue syndrome is a mysterious disorder of unknown origin which causes chronic debilitating fatigue, headache, depression, and muscle weakness. One user who had been diagnosed with Epstein Barr Virus which is a form of chronic fatigue syndrome, found that medical marijuana has made a substantial difference in energy levels and motivation. He reported that his regular daily use of marijuana allowed him to live a normal life without the symptoms of his illness being present.

There have to date been very few satisfactory studies to determine the effects of treating this disorder with medical marijuana.

## Chronic pain

Chronic pain has been treated for decades using opioid narcotics, including morphine and oxycodone. Opiates are highly addictive and patients are able to build a tolerance, requiring increased dosages and greater risk of side effects or even accidental overdose. More potent opiates cause many patients to become too heavily medicated while others are found to not be strong enough, as is often the case with new non-addictive synthetics entering the market. Liver damage is also often a concern when taking opiates.

Chronic pain from advanced cancer is well treated with the use of medical marijuana and studies have documented such.

Cannabinoids block pain pathways similar to opiates, but use a different neurochemical signaling system. Patients experience various degrees of relief for different symptoms. After using medical marijuana some patients stop taking opiates finding the medical marijuana works as good or better for them without the side effects of opiates.

## Depression

When depression gets to the level which it becomes clinical depression it is a serious illness. Clinical depression is a long term, debilitating illness which can result in a patient becoming suicidal. This illness is usually treated with MAO inhibitor drugs such as Prozac. Depression can also effect and be a secondary condition to people suffering from AIDS, Hepatitis C, Cancer and other serious and life threatening illnesses.

Studies have clearly shown that patients using cannabis to treat Hepatitis C, MS, AIDS, cancer, and other diseases have reported reduced depression.

Since early times cannabis has been known for its mood elevating and psychoactive characteristics. In the medical textbooks of the early twentieth-century, cannabis is listed as a treatment for depression. Cannabis's synthetic relative, Marinol although not labeled as an anti-depressant has successfully been used to treat bi-polar and clinical depression.

Cannabis can also have negative side effects on patients who suffer from psychiatric and mood disorders including irritability, loss of motivation or ambition, paranoia, and so on.  So, patients are strongly urged to discuss the possibility of medical marijuana use with their doctor so that it may be correctly monitored.

Anti-euphoric or dysphoric reactions have been reported in some studies of cannabis, especially among older patients who are not used to the euphoric producing capabilities of cannabis.

Another study at McGill University in Montreal shows that cannabis is effective against depression in moderate doses and that long term or heavy use only makes depression worse.  The result of that study was that excessive cannabis use in people suffering from depression leads to a high risk of psychosis.  Surveys have also shown that marijuana use among adolescents is a risk factor for depression.

The results of numerous studies has clearly shown that people with mental disorders such as depression, anxiety, and other associated ailments are more likely to use alcohol, tobacco, and other drugs.  The big question lies in what extent marijuana may exacerbate their problem and to what extent it is a valid form of self-treatment for their illness.

## Diabetes

Diabetes is excess blood sugar levels due to insufficient production of insulin by the body. Cannabis has shown to be effective in treating severe nausea, appetite loss, pain and other symptomatic relief associated with diabetes. There have not been adequate studies conducted to determine whether cannabis can effect disease progression. *Diabetes- see also- Autoimmune inflammatory diseases*

## Dystonia

Dystonia is generally classified as a movement disorder. It is characterized by involuntary contractions as well as painful tension in the muscles. There have been documented studies which now show that medical cannabis can be used effectively in the treatment of Dystonia and its symptoms.

## Epilepsy

Epilepsy is related to the misfiring of brain cells, resulting in a seizure. These seizures can include convulsions, loss of consciousness, loss of coordination, confused sensory states and even death.

There are several origins of epilepsy be it disease, genetics or a serious accident or injury. Currently epilepsy is treated with a variety of drugs and is treated with great success with conventional medications. There are still a small percentage of patients who cannot find satisfactory relief in treating their illness.

Cannabis has been found to be highly effective in treating grand mal epilepsy, patients have reported that they are able to use cannabis and completely eliminate seizures in conjunction with their regular medicine and in some cases without.

Cannabis has also been highly effective in treating complex partial seizure disorders, again patients find they are able to eliminate seizures altogether with cannabis use.

Care must be taken to understand that marijuana is not a cure for epilepsy and cannabis has not been proven effective in treating patients of petit mal or absence seizures and in fact one study recently showed evidence that CBD may reduce or counteract the effectiveness of other drugs used to treat petit mal.
Epilepsy patients should use great care when ingesting THC orally, as patients may be more susceptible to seizures when they withdraw from long term oral treatment. Patients should reduce doses with the guidance of their doctor.

## Epstein Barr Virus
See chronic fatigue

## Eye disorders

See glaucoma

## Fibromyalgia

See Arthritis

## Gastrointestinal disorders

Medical marijuana has now become more accepting in treating gastrointestinal disorders such as colitis, irritable bowel syndrome, and Crohn's disease with Cannabis. All these disorders produce painful gastrointestinal cramping and inflammation, chronic pain, diarrhea and also result in weight loss. Patients have consistently reported relief from the use of cannabis to treat these symptoms.

Recent studies have shown that CB1 and CB2 receptors act to suppress gastrointestinal cramping, acid reflux, inflammation, and intestinal secretions.

## Glaucoma

Glaucoma is best described as a disease causing an excess buildup of fluid pressure in the eye. After time, this pressure will permanently damage the optic nerve, leading to a progressive loss of vision and eventually complete blindness.

Glaucoma is found to be the leading cause in America of blindness and effects two million people over the age of 35 in this country. The physical side effects of this disease can include acute attacks with severe headaches and nausea. Halos or blindspots eventually become the most prominent symptoms. Glaucoma is treated with conventional drugs and also surgery.

The discovery of the benefits of cannabis use in glaucoma patients dates way back to early 1970. It was discovered around this time that cannabis could help alleviate and control glaucoma. A UCLA study was conducted and confirmed that cannabis caused a significant reduction in intraocular pressure in patients. This finding was likewise backed up by other studies from other leading schools.

Cannabis was found to produce a consistent reduction in IOP of approximately 20%-30% for a period of approximately four hours. Heavier doses were not found to have any effect in further reducing IOP levels in any greater amount.

The first patient in the US ever to receive medical marijuana from the government back in the 1970's suffered from glaucoma. This guy, whose name was Robert Randall claimed marijuana was able to prevent him from losing his eyesight. The government eventually raided his garden and Randall literally sued the US government for the right to treat his disease with cannabis and won. The government was forced to supply him with free medical marijuana and Randall technically became a test subject for the FDA. This program grew to approximately 30 patients, many of which suffered from glaucoma who had made their way through the mountain of paperwork to gain access to government issued cannabis. The government compassion program was killed by the senior Bush administration.

Cannabis has been found to be most effective for wide-angle glaucoma. It is reported not to respond effectively in treating narrow or closed angle glaucoma although patients find cannabis helps to manage pain from attacks.

In Jamaica, a product known as canasol® has been on the market since the 1980's and is used to treat glaucoma. Canasol comes in an eyedropper bottle and are drops applied directly into the eye. Efforts are underway here to develop a similar product.

Glaucoma does not seem to respond well to oral doses and is best to be smoked by glaucoma patients. It has also been reported that lower grade marijuana is just as effective in treatment as higher grade marijuana in relieving IOP. Some have actually reported to achieve greater success with lower grade cannabis.

Patients who suffer from other eye disorders not involving IOP have also reported success with cannabis, such is the case with retinitis, which is classified as an inflammation of the retina or macular degeneration, the deterioration of the retina, also optic nerve hypoplasia, an under development of the eye which impairs vision.  Even people who are colorblind have actually reported seeing colors ranging from minimal to vibrant after consuming cannabis.

## Hangover

Cannabis has been found to alleviate the symptoms associated with hangovers, including nausea, stomach discomfort, and headache.

## Hepatitis C

Hepatitis C is an infection spread through blood which effects the liver, common with IV drug users and people who have had tattoos.  Over time, this disease will eventually destroy the liver, usually resulting in the necessity for liver transplant.

Researchers at the University of California in San Francisco found that marijuana dramatically improves the effects of hepatitis C treatment.  That study examined over 70 patients taking the most common prescription treatment for hepatitis C, the anti-viral drugs ribavirin and interferon.  The severe side effects of these drugs include nausea, loss of appetite, fatigue and depression.  The regime of treatment is so extreme that many patients drop out.  In this study, after six months, 86% of the cannabis users had successfully completed treatment where only 59% of the non-cannabis users completed treatment.  Further 54% of the cannabis users showed a substantial virological response with no signs of the virus , six months following treatment.  This compared to only 18% of the non-cannabis group who achieved such results.

Cannabis is routinely used with hepatitis C patients to combat the appetite and weight loss, reduce depression, fatigue associated with the illness, and better cope with the rigorous treatment of conventional drugs.

Be aware that patients in liver transport programs have been kicked out and allowed to die for using cannabis.  Liver transplant candidates are required to submit to routine urine testing.

## Insomnia

Marijuana, particularly the concentrated dose known as "hashish" has great benefits in treating insomnia and sleeplessness.  Medical studies have outright proven that THC & CBD, two properties in cannabis help improve sleep. Cannabis will generally energize you for the first hour or so after smoking, then will gradually become more sedative.

## Lou Gehrig 's disease (ALS)

Amyotrophic lateral sclerosis (ALS) occurs sporadically in people without any known cause.  It is generally characterized by the ongoing loss of motor neurons in the brain, spinal cord, and the peripheral nervous system.

There are approximately 30,000 Americans living today with ALS.

Animal studies and other research has shown that cannaboids can actually slow disease progression and prolong patients survival with this illness. Many doctors are consistently and routinely recommending medical marijuana to people suffering from ALS.

Cannabis has been found to be effective in treating and alleviating pain and muscle spasm associated with ALS. Studies have also found that medical marijuana use results in improved appetite, helps combat depression, and helps to control uncontrollable drooling associated with ALS by drying up saliva in the mouth.

## Menstrual disorders
See PMS

## Migraine
Migraine is a chronic disorder which results in painful, severe headaches which are often accompanied by nausea and which can last for hours. Migraines affect 20% of the American population. Cannabis has been proven to be highly effective in treating migraine headaches. There have not been any extensive studies done on record as to the effect of medical marijuana use on migraine condition.

However, one independent study has concluded that chronic marijuana use might suppress the user's susceptibility to migraines.

## Morning sickness
See pregnancy

## Multiple sclerosis
This is a chronic and relapsing neuro-degenerative disease in which the brain and spinal cord nerves become progressively damaged by the destruction of the protective tissue that coats them. Patients have reported painful neuropathic pain and muscle spasm, loss of coordination and balance, numbness, impaired vision, tremors, and weakness. Approximately 200 people, usually between the ages of 20 and 40, are diagnosed with multiple sclerosis each week in the US.

Montel Williams is one celebrity suffering from MS who openly admitted that it was the only thing that worked for him. In fact, he claims its use allows him to enjoy a productive life despite suffering from MS.

Numerous studies have been done documenting the ability of marijuana to reduce or relieve symptoms associated with MS. These symptoms include pain, depression, fatigue, bladder incontinence, and more.

If that doesn't sound promising how about this. A Harvard University study done by the brilliant medical cannabis pioneer, noted Professor Dr. Lester Grinspoon. Reported a case where an MS patient who was severely debilitated by his MS regained his ability to walk, run, speak, and engage in sexual activity, all things he had lost after being treated with medical marijuana.

Recent studies are showing that cannabis can actually inhibit the progression of MS and migrate its symptoms.

## Pregnancy

The use of any drug, including alcohol and tobacco is not recommended during pregnancy. However, it has been shown that medical marijuana use during pregnancy poses no health risks to the unborn fetus. There is no reason why medical marijuana could not be used for severe morning sickness when recommended and supervised by a licensed physician.

Marijuana has not been shown to cause birth defects or have a reverse negative effect on an unborn child. Studies have now dispelled concerns that marijuana use causes fetal alcohol syndrome and other birth defects.

A major study conducted in Jamaica found improved development in children born to mothers who used marijuana during pregnancy.

The therapeutic value of medical marijuana must be weighed against the hypothetical risks. Many woman find cannabis highly effective in relieving morning sickness.

*Breast feeding*
THC is fat-soluble and a small trace amount makes its way into the mother's breast milk. Studies have discovered that a fraction of one percent of a mothers dose of THC might be delivered to the baby through breast feeding. Another study found no effect of marijuana exposure on infant development.

## Pre-Menstrual Syndrome (PMS)

Medical marijuana has been found to be highly effective at alleviating the pain & discomfort associated with PMS. It is well documented that woman have reported relief for cramps, tension, headaches and dysphoria or dysmenorrhea by using cannabis. Cannabis is also effective in treating endometriosis, which is an inflammation of the uterine lining. In fact, dysmenorrhea was commonly treated with cannabis in the nineteenth century and even Queen Victoria's personal physician prescribed it to the queen. History shows that as far back as the 1800's, women were commonly using cannabis for menstrual cramps, labor pains, and childbirth.

Some strains of medical cannabis are specifically recommended to help alleviate these symptoms, i.e.

Catalyst, Neptune Kush, Skittles, etc. A knowledgeable and reputable dispensary will be able to recommend something as new strains are being created daily. Indica strains have been said to work well.

In modern medical history, doctors have prescribed anti-depressants and tranquillizers for severe PMS. However, as a safe alternative to this, doctors are now recommending medical cannabis for this ailment.

## Rheumatism
See arthritis

## Skin diseases
Cannabis has been found to effectively relieve pruritis and other certain skin conditions. Several physicians are actually now recommending cannabis to treat eczema and psoriasis.
Studies have also found success using topical skin applications of cannabinoids and endocannabinoids. Likely the result of the anti-inflammatory properties of Cannabis.

## Spinal cord injuries
Medical marijuana has enjoyed great success in treating patients suffering from spinal cord injury. Symptoms usually associated with spinal cord injuries include chronic pain, muscle spasm, and includes paralysis of the legs, or

both legs and arms. Patients have found cannabis effectively relieves spasticity and pain.

Typically spinal cord injury patients are prescribed a heavy treatment consisting of opiates, tranquilizers and other highly addictive drugs. Many patients have reported that they have outright eliminated those drugs through treatment exclusively with medical marijuana. Many report even better results in effectively controlling their pain and other symptoms.

It is so recognized for its effectiveness that some hospitals actually allow marijuana to be smoked by paraplegics and quadriplegics in their wards. This including some V.A. hospitals.

The response to treatment by medical marijuana for spinal cord injuries has been greatly promising and is being well documented.

## Stroke

We have certainly established that cannabinoids have neuroprotective properties against brain and nerve cell damage. There is still little studies into the effects of cannabis with stroke victims. Several patients have successfully controlled symptoms related to post stoke damage and injury.

## Tardive dyskinesia

Tardive dyskinesia is a disorder with characteristics of involuntarily chewing and darting of the tongue. It has been associated to the long term use of antipychotic drugs. Cannabis is not recommended for the treatment and extremely limited research if any has been done on the effects of cannabis on this disorder.


## Tourette's syndrome

Tourette's syndrome is a neuro-psychiatric disorder which is familiarly characterized by facial twitches and often profane vocal fits. Its cause remains unknown and its severity varies.

Studies have shown that THC ingested orally has been shown to significantly improve the symptoms in TS patient's. Results show reductions in severity and obsessive compulsive behavior.

# Understanding cannabinoids
## marijuana's properties

There are a total of 483 distinct and identified organic chemical components that are scientifically proven to exist in the marijuana plant. Components like sugars, proteins, and amino acids are all very common in all vegetation forms. But there are a total of 66 components that exist only in the marijuana plant and nowhere else in the universe. The most notable being THC, CBC and CBN. Each of these types also has subclasses.

DELTA-9 THC *scientifically known as delta-9 tetrahydrocannabinol*, is the main psychoactive ingredient in marijuana. THC is present in all cannabis in varying amounts. THC is the property that also stimulates appetite.

CBC *scientifically known as cannabichromine* remains inactive in its pure form and is suspected of making THC increasing potent.

CBN *scientifically known as cannabinol*, is created through the degration of THC and is extremely weaker in the psychoactive value, approximately about 10% of THC's value. CBN appears to potentiate the disorienting qualities of THC.

CBD *scientifically known as cannabidiol* is present in most cannabis strains and vary from very small amounts to 95%.

CBD possesses antibiotic, analgestic, and sedative properties.  CBD has been found to increase the depressant effect and regulate the euphoric effect.  CBD contributes to by interacting with THC to potentate various elements.

CBG *scientifically known as cannabigerol* possess antibiotic qualities and is a non psychoactive cannabinoid element that is believed to reduce intraocular pressure (IOP).

Hemp farming in this country came to a sudden halt in 1937 when Congress passed the Marihuana Tax Act. However, in 1942, thousands of farmers grew hemp for the war effort under encouragement by the US Government yielding their "Hemp for Victory" slogan. When the war ended so did the governments allowance to grow once more and this was the last time in this countries history hemp farming was allowed under federal law.

One of the greatest myths out there is that the United States Constitution and Declaration of Independence were both written on hemp paper. Until 1883, approximately 90% of all paper was derived from hemp. Historians report that even the bible was written on hemp paper. Hemp was used to print money, stocks, and bonds. It was also used to write the first two drafts of the Constitution. Hemp was however, not used for the actual Constitution or Declaration of Independence, parchment was. On July 19, 1776 Congress ordered the Declaration to be copied and engrossed from its July 2nd second draft on Dutch hemp paper onto parchment which was then signed by the signors on August 2, 1776.

Many of this countries founding fathers including Washington and Jefferson were hemp farmers who manufactured rope, sails and paper from hemp. Our countries early settlers used hemp for lamp oil and many early colonies made hemp cultivation compulsory saying that the production of hemp was necessary for the wealth and protection of the country.

Hemp is one of a variety of the plant, Cannabis Sativa. Its actual Tetrahydrocannabinol or THC content is less than 1%. THC is the component in Cannabis which creates the "high" or psychoactive quality associated with the plant. More than thirty nations currently allow hemp production and its use as fiber and even food dates back more than 10,000 years. Today Hemp can produce textile, clothing, paper, plastic, paint, cosmetics and health care, animal feed, insulation, foodstuffs and more.

The medical field is now praising the nutritional value of hemp seed, and the fact it is only second to soy beans in protein and that hemp seeds contain the highest natural concentration of essential amino and fatty acids known to man.

*"Hemp has the potential to create more than 25,000 environmentally friendly products"*
- **Popular Mechanics Magazine**

Hemp is currently grown for commercial and industrial use in thirty countries, including Canada, Japan and Europe.

Hemp produces higher yields than its counterpart cotton and only takes 100 days to cultivate and harvest.

However, only the DEA has the power to permit hemp farming in this country, and continues to deny every permit within the past 40 years. The DEA does allow importing of hemp products certified to be THC free. This includes clothing, beauty products and even some food products. Sterilized hemp seed, like those found in some bird seed are also allowed.

Despite several states enacting laws to explore hemp cultivation options and research, the DEA has threatened to arrest any farmers who try and grow hemp. Some states have actually now enacted legislation to license farmers to grow hemp.

Early Hemp farming in Kentucky

# Federal Marijuana Laws

The federal government regulates and controls drugs under the Controlled Substance Act (CSA) (21 U.S.C. 811) which does not define or recognize the difference between recreational and medical use of marijuana.  These laws generally focus on larger amounts of marijuana, with special interest in cases which cross state lines or international borders.

The federal government ranks drugs on a schedule and access to every drug relies on its assigned schedule. Marijuana falls under the most restrictive of all, schedule 1. This ranking is reserved for drugs which are considered highly addictive and lack any medical benefit.

In the late 1970's, 35 states passed legislation to establish medical marijuana research programs and each program was systematically ransacked by federal drug regulations. Because of this marijuana research was left unchartered.

In 1972, NORML started a lawsuit against the government to change marijuana to a schedule two drug.  This resulted in a lawsuit that ran nearly twenty years with the government prevailing at the end.

In 1988, a DEA Administrative Judge ruled that marijuana had benefits clear beyond question and that it should be reclassified as a schedule two drug.  That ruling was overruled by DEA Chief, John Lawn claiming it would send the wrong message about marijuana's harmfulness.

Technically doctors are prohibited from prescribing marijuana for medical use under federal law, but under the power of the First Amendment they can "recommend" its use for medical treatment.

Federal agents, like those with the Drug Enforcement Agency (DEA) can currently use the "Controlled Substance Act" to arrest patients for its cultivation, use, and possession.
It is common known fact that the DEA and Attorney General's office have exaggerated plant numbers and inflammatory rhetoric to go after patients and growers in all states.

Federal marijuana laws are very severe and carry drastic consequences if convicted. In several federal cases, judges have ruled that medical use cannot be entered or used as a defense. A good example of this was the federal case against Ed Rosenthal in California (*US v. Rosenthal, 2003*). Ed was banned in his defense from using the fact that he was cultivating marijuana legally under state law for medical patients, not only that, but Ed had additionally been deputized by the City of Oakland to grow medical marijuana. None of these facts were allowed to be brought up at Ed's trial. The jury found out about this and recanted their guilty verdict.

There are currently two federal sentencing laws, sentencing guidelines which were enacted by the U.S. Sentencing Commission and the mandatory sentencing guidelines which were enacted by congress. The current mandatory minimums were drafted in the 1986 drug bill. They take into account how much marijuana defendants were in possession of, and any prior convictions the defendant may have. Every marijuana conviction under the guidelines is eligible for jail time, and a minimum of 85% of that sentence must be served.

In the January 2005 decision of *U.S. v Booker*, a Supreme Court decided that the federal sentencing guidelines are advisory and no longer mandatory. Despite this decision there are mandatory minimums which primarily target offenses involving large amounts of marijuana. There is a five-year mandatory sentencing for cultivating 100 plants or 100 Kgs, a ten-year mandatory sentence if the defendant has a prior felony drug conviction, up to life if the defendant has two prior felony convictions.

Although under the current Obama administration, the DEA and Justice Department have publically gone on record saying that they have no interest in pursuing individual patients, but only large traffickers. Facts remain that Obama's numbers average the same as Bush's. The Obama Administration has conducted over 100 raids and prosecuted 46 people for medical marijuana related offenses. They also appear to now be taking a negative position towards the medical marijuana industry. In other words, everything he promised to do in support of patients' rights to access medical marijuana has turned out to be lies. Very recently behind this administration, there has been very aggressive action towards medical marijuana dispensaries, caregivers, and grower's. Also in the Obama Administration path has been landlords who rent space to medical marijuana businesses. They have now been threatened with asset forfeiture and even arrest.

What the future for medical marijuana on a federal level it is totally unpredictable. Right now, it's looking like patient's and especially medical marijuana businesses are in for a very rocky ride. I see businesses being eliminated and patients continued access through exclusive one on one caregivers or self-cultivation. There will always be an underground of sources for patients, but the high profile commercial aspect of it may soon be a thing of the past. If there is any future for dispensaries it may be selective on who can, or can afford to qualify. There will be government regulation that is very strict, and licensing fees may be cost prohibitive for independent business?

Still at this time under federal law, marijuana has no medicinal value and remains on the most dangerous list. Possession, cultivation, and use are all illegal under federal law. The DEA is a federal agency created in 1973 under the Nixon Administration. to establish a single government entity to combat "an all-out global war on the drug menace." In the beginning in 1973 the DEA encompassed 1,470 Special Agents and a budget of less than $75 million. Today, the DEA employs about 5,000 Special Agents and has a budget of approximately $2.02 billion.

## Asset Forfeiture

Federal Laws allow for the seizure and forfeiture of property and assets obtained through or used in connection of a felony drug offense. Prosecutors are pressured to include forfeiture offenses in all drug indictments. Although, highly rare and very unlikely, this can also apply to landlords who rent to marijuana patients and growers.

Dispensary operators, growers, and caregivers all should consult with an attorney regarding protections which may be available to you to protect your assets from forfeiture.

## Landlord/Tenant

Under the terms of most rental leases, the landlord can sometimes even without proper notice, have access to enter your dwelling. Access is usually required to inspect the property for maintenance necessity, or enter for pest control, etc. The landlord may usually have the right to enter your place without notice in the case of an emergency.

Never honor any request that you not be present when your landlord needs access to your property. Landlords do not have any right to exclude you or any other party listed on the lease, short of proper eviction proceedings.

Having a home security system usually deters a landlord from entering your property without giving proper, advanced notice. However, this can backfire on you if you are cultivating plants and your alarm goes off and triggers a response from police and your plants are discovered.

Some leases now, especially in California include prohibitions on the use and cultivation of drugs, that including medical marijuana. The best policy is to just be as indiscreet as possible about your marijuana use and especially if you are cultivating on your property. Laws in several states point out that cultivation must be in an enclosed, locked facility. Your closet is technically an enclosed, locked facility as long as there is at least one lockable door separating you from general public access. A lockable front door would certainly provide a locked facility, provided you have no roommates. A secured lock on the door of wherever you are cultivating your plants, (i.e. bedroom, basement) would be a locked facility if you have other roommates.

## Operating a vehicle under the influence of marijuana

A person is guilty of a DUI if they operate a motor vehicle while under the influence of alcohol and/or drugs, OR operates a motor vehicle as an habitual user of any controlled substance. Colo. Rev. Stat. Ann. § 42-4-1301(1)(a)-(c) (West 2010).

### The Affirmative Defense

The fact that any person charged is or has been entitled to use one or more drugs under the laws of this state, including, but not limited to, the medical use of marijuana shall not constitute a defense against any charge of violating this subsection. *Id.* § 42-4-1301(1)(e).

### Implied Consent

- A person who drives a motor vehicle upon the streets and highways and elsewhere throughout this state shall be required to take and complete, and to cooperate in the taking and completing of, any test or tests of the person's breath or blood when so requested and directed by a law enforcement officer having probable cause to believe that the person was driving a motor vehicle in violation of the prohibitions against DUI, DUI per se, DWAI, habitual user, or UDD. *Id.* § 42-4-1301.1(2)(a)(I).
- If a person refuses to take or to complete any test or tests and such person subsequently stands trial for DUI or DWAI, the refusal to take or to complete, or to cooperate with the completing of, any test or tests shall be admissible into evidence at the trial. *Id.* § 42-4-1301(6)(a)(III)(d).

- Neither the results of such *preliminary screening* test nor the fact that the person refused such test shall be used in any court action except in a hearing outside of the presence of a jury, when such hearing is held to determine if a law enforcement officer had probable cause to believe that the driver committed a violation of this section. The results of such preliminary screening test shall be made available to the driver or the driver's attorney on request. *Id.* § 42-4-1301 (6)(h)(i)(III).
- The department shall revoke the license of a person for refusal of test for one year for a first refusal, two years for a second refusal of test and three years for a third or subsequent refusal. *Id.* § 42-2-126(3)(c)(I).
- Generally, an arrested person has no right to consult with an attorney before taking a chemical test. *Drake v. Colorado Dept. of Revenue, Motor Vehicle Div.*, 674 P.2d 359 (1984).
- When an arresting officer invokes the sanctions of the implied consent law by requesting the driver to submit to chemical testing, the officer has a corresponding duty to comply with the driver's request for a blood test. *People v. Gillett*, 629 P.2d 613 (1981).

## Penalties

- First offense (DUI, DUI per se, or habitual user) - imprisonment in the county jail for a mandatory minimum of five days but no more than one year; fine of at least six hundred dollars, but no more than one thousand dollars; at least forty-eight hours but no more than ninety-six hours of useful public service; the court may impose a period of probation that shall not exceed two years, which probation may include any conditions permitted by law. *Id.* § 42-4-1307(3).

- First offense (DWAI)* - imprisonment in the county jail for a mandatory minimum of two days but no more than one hundred eighty days; fine of at least two hundred dollars but no more than five hundred dollars; at least twenty-four hours but no more than forty-eight hours of useful public service; the court may impose a period of probation that shall not exceed two years, which probation may include any conditions permitted by law. *Id.* § 42-4-1307(4).
  - \* "Driving while ability impaired" or "DWAI" means driving a motor vehicle when a person has consumed alcohol, one or more drugs, or a combination of both, that affects the person to the *slightest degree* which fails to meet the level for DUI impairment. There is only a sentencing disparity when it comes to the first offense. After the first DUI or DWAI each subsequent DUI or DWAI is punished without distinction.
- Second offense - imprisonment in the county jail for a mandatory minimum ten consecutive days but no more than one year; fine of at least six hundred dollars but no more than one thousand five hundred dollars; at least forty-eight hours but no more than one hundred twenty hours of useful public service; a period of probation of at least two years. *Id.* § 42-4-1307(5).
- Third and subsequent offense - imprisonment in the county jail for a mandatory minimum of sixty consecutive days but no more than one year; mandatory participation in a court-ordered alcohol

and drug driving safety education or treatment program; fine of at least six hundred dollars but no more than one thousand five hundred dollars; at least forty-eight hours but no more than one hundred twenty hours of useful public service; a period of probation of at least two years. *Id.* § 42-4-1307(6).

## Sobriety Checkpoints

Sobriety checkpoints are permissible in Colorado under both the state and federal Constitution.

- In light of the state's substantial interest in combating drunk driving, sobriety checkpoint was not "unreasonable" under Fourth Amendment. The stops averaged no longer than three minutes and were found to be a relatively minor burden on motorists. Checkpoint was held permissible when officer did not stop vehicles that turned around to avoid checkpoint. *People v. Rister*, 803 P.2d 483 (Col. 1990).

## Case Law

*Stanger v. Colorado Dept. of Revenue, Motor Vehicle Div., State of Colo.*, 780 P.2d 64 (1989) -- An arresting officer has the discretion to demand a driver to submit to tests in order to reveal the presence of drugs if driver is suspected of DUI-drug offense. The driver has no right to choose which test.

*Cox v. People*, 735 P.2d 153 (1987) -- Since driver may have reason for refusing to submit to test that is unrelated to consciousness of guilt, inference of intoxication that is permissible from evidence of driver's refusal to take blood or breath test is rebuttable.

*Drake v. Colorado Dept. of Revenue, Motor Vehicle Div.*, 674 P.2d 359 (1984) -- Generally, an arrested person has no right to consult with an attorney before taking a chemical test. If a defendant refuses to consent to testing before talking to an attorney, such behavior will generally be deemed a refusal.

*Halter v. Department of Revenue of State of Colo., Motor Vehicle Div.,* 857 P.2d 535 (1993) - Officers' request that driver undergo drug testing was reasonable where breath test showed no presence of alcohol but driver displayed various indications of intoxication. If an officer has probable cause to supported arrest and breath alcohol test, officer also may request that driver submit to drug test. If driver passes the breath test, drug use is a reasonable explanation for driver's intoxication regardless of whether other evidence existed to support search for drugs.

*Dayhoff v. State, Motor Vehicle Division*, 595 P.2d 1051 (1979) -- Driver not driving on public highway is not controlled by implied consent statute. Driver may refuse test without license suspension.

*Thompson v. People*, 510 P.2d 311 (1979) -- Standard of proof for DUI is "substantially under the influence," rather than intoxication to the "slightest degree". The degree of intoxication must be substantial so as to render one incapable of safely operating a vehicle.

## Talking with your lawyer about marijuana

Attorney's and their clients enjoy "attorney/client confidentiality". This means that an attorney generally will not, or cannot be made to disclose any incriminating evidence against their client. There is one exception to this rule and that is in the case of a crime which will be committed in the future. If you run into trouble because you are exercising your right as a recreational user or medical marijuana patient, be up front and honest with your attorney. You have a legal defense at state level.

Always consult an attorney if you face legal issues with your medical marijuana consumption. You can still be prosecuted and do jail time at state level for certain infractions. When speaking with your attorney be discreet discussing revenue from your garden, or sales of marijuana.

## Interaction with Law Enforcement

When the cops start mouthing off about all the charges they're going to slap you with and all the jail time you are going to do. Remember this; the prosecutor is the only person who can actually charge you with a crime(s). The police make recommendations through their police report. On occasion they will plant evidence or directly misrepresent facts on their report. There are good cops, ones who may be compassionate about medical marijuana use and even support recreational use. Others will outright lie and use every deceptive trick in the book to get you to open your mouth and hopefully say the wrong thing. They are literally trained and experienced at being deceptive. "Everything you say, can and will be used against you in a court of law". If you are in a group, the members of the group need to all evoke their right to counsel and keep their mouths shut. A common police practice is to quickly separate the parties and attempt to turn them against each other through lies and misrepresentations. Hold your ground as a group. The police are likely not really your friends; they're probably not going to help you. Most are going to trap you by letting you talk. You can incriminate yourself by rattling on, or even with a single word. In every aspect police should be considered the enemy of marijuana and the medical marijuana patient or recreational user. They have the power to confiscate your stash, although this may be challengeable later in court. I know in California and other states, police have been ordered by the court to return confiscated medical marijuana and have been found liable for damages in civil actions for destroying medical marijuana or plants. Courts in other states have upheld that returning medicine subjects the police to federal arrest.

Police and their agents do not have to admit they are police officers.

*FACT: undercover cops can get hazard pay for doing drugs as part of their cover*

If you have an encounter with law enforcement DO NOT CONSENT TO A SEARCH, DO NOT ANSWER ANY QUESTIONS. If you are arrested, IMMEDIATELY EVOKE YOUR RIGHT TO COUNSEL! Remain calm and be polite.
DO NOT SIGN ANY STATEMENT
DO NOT VOLUNTEER ANY INFORMATION
DO NOT PHYSICALLY RESIST

Exercising your right to counsel
evokes rights which protect you!

There are three basic types of encounters with police: 1) conversation 2) detention and 3) arrest

## Conversation

When police are trying to get information from you, but do not have enough evidence to detain or arrest you, they will attempt to get you to say something to incriminate yourself. This may seem like a "friendly or casual" encounter.

## Detention

You can only be detained by police if they establish "reasonable suspicion". Even though you are not technically arrested, you cannot leave. Detention is only for a short period and police are not supposed to move you. You can be patted down and any bag you are carrying could be searched for the purpose of making sure you do not have a weapon. If in the process the police happen to find a half ounce of marijuana or stolen credit cards, you can then be charged with that. Police are not supposed to reach into your pockets unless they feel a weapon. At this point ask the police to verify that you are being detained. If they say no, then leave. If they say you are being detained, inform them you wish to say nothing further without your lawyer present.

## Arrest

You can only be arrested if the police have established probable cause that you are involved in a crime. Once you are arrested the police can thoroughly search you, your automobile, and any belongings you have there.

REMAIN SILENT, DO NOT RESIST, AND DO NOT ANSWER ANY QUESTIONS.

Once you express your right to counsel, the police are supposed to stop questioning you.

You are entitled to make a phone call when you are arrested.  Don't expect to do that when you get to the jail.  It may be quite a while before you are allowed to actually get to make that call, be patient.

Phones at jails often only make collect calls and ALL PHONE CONVERSATIONS BY PEOPLE IN CUSTODY CAN BE MONITORED.  Do not discuss sensitive matters on police phones, always assumed that they are being monitored.

REASONABLE SUSPICION

Black's Law Dictionary defines reasonable suspicion as "*a particularized and objective basis, supported by specific and articulable facts, for suspecting a person of criminal activity*".  Police cannot base reasonable suspicion solely on a hunch.  You cannot be stopped because you appear to fit the profile of someone who smokes marijuana.

The rule of thumb is, police can pretty much stop you for anything and do anything they want.  It's going to be your word against theirs and who do you think is going to be the one they believe?  My advice is to avoid any kind of police attention.  Be a good neighbor, keep your stereo down, don't throw wild parties, and certainly don't piss anyone off who may even suspect you have or are growing medical marijuana. Use common sense, don't stand out, act mature, and just fit in. Be there for the medical marijuana cause and rallies but on the outside be "Joe Average Law abiding Guy" and attract as little attention as possible.

## PROBABLE CAUSE

Probable cause is when a police officer has observed something which would indicate a crime has been committed and which would give that officer the right to conduct a search without consent. Let's take a look at an example of how this would take effect. You are pulled over and the officer notes the distinctive odor of burned marijuana permeating from the inside of your automobile, that officer has now established probable cause to believe there is marijuana in the car and may search the car without obtaining your consent.

## PLAIN VIEW DOCTRINE

The plain view doctrine allows a police officer to search without consent when he or she observes something in plain view which would indicate criminal behavior. Let's take an example of this. You are pulled over and as the officer approaches the car and asks for your license, he notices a roach in your ashtray. Under the "plain view doctrine" he has now established the ability to perform a search of your vehicle. The empty beer can on the floor in back, the pack of rolling papers sitting on the console, the joint tucked above your ear that you forgot about. All of these are examples of things that can trigger a search under the "plain view doctrine".


## SEARCHES

We have addressed two incidences where police can search your car without consent. One is probable cause and the second is under the "Plain View Doctrine". Another way which we haven't addressed yet is by obtaining a search warrant. A search warrant is an order signed by a judge, usually a magistrate judge who gives police permission to search your house, property, or a certain area of land or property. A search warrant is obtained when an officer appears before a judge with an affidavit and establishes to the judge that there is reason to believe criminal activity or evidence of criminal activity is occurring or present at that location. Let's look at an example of this. A person comes into your house. During this time he observes both you selling marijuana to people and a large amount of marijuana in your house. This person turns out to be either an undercover cop or a police informant. The guy comes back another day and wants to buy some marijuana from you and you sell it to him. Hey it can happen, when I was working for Dennis Peron at the San Francisco Cannabis Buyers Club, Dennis met these two guys who claimed to be from out of town and were caregivers for a bunch of medical marijuana patients and who had been wanting to open up their own medical marijuana dispensary. Dennis sold them two pounds and they were actually undercover cops. So undercover cops are out there victimizing medical marijuana users.

The other way that police can search is to obtain your consent or the consent of another adult residing at a residence. In other words your roommate not knowing any better can let the police right in to find the plants you are growing in the basement. Take the time to educate anyone living at your residence to never consent to police searches. IF THE POLICE DO TRY AND SEARCH YOUR HOUSE, CAR, OR BACKPACK, IMMEDIATELY OBJECT TO THE SEARCH. Say "*I do not consent to this search and it is being done without my consent*". This may not stop them from continuing but if you are searched illegally, they may not be able to use any evidence they find against you.

Dennis Peron, who is by far the father of medical marijuana was in Utah with some friends and staying at a hotel. Someone from the hotel called police after smelling the odor of marijuana coming from their hotel room into the hotel's hallway. The police came and knocked on the door announcing themselves as police officers. Dennis exited the room but knew enough to lock the door right behind him as he walked into the hallway. Dennis refused to give consent to a search, the police went in anyway, found his pot and arrested him. Even though it was a nightmare and cost

Dennis a good deal in attorney fees and time, the case eventually had to be dismissed after it was decided that the pot could not be entered into evidence because it had been obtained through an illegal search.

Watch out for what is referred to as "casual consent". If you are stopped by police and get out of your car but leave your driver's door ajar, or say "I'd rather you didn't search" they can search and claim that you "reluctantly" give them permission for the search

## Trash

It is important to point out that the U.S. Supreme Court has ruled that you have no expectancy for trash which you have put out for collection. This means that police and other law enforcement agencies have a right to retrieve your trash and go through it looking for evidence to use against you. A good shredder, which cross shreds for added security is recommended.

## USA PATRIOT ACT

In 2001 immediately following the 9/11 attacks, congress quickly passed the Patriot Act. It allows the government to intercept personal telephone conversations and emails and to investigate financial, medical, and library records without obtaining a warrant. Consequently, it also allows the government to investigate you, under the disguise that you may be a terrorist.  Let's look at statistics, from 763 warrantless wiretaps conducted under the Patriot Act in 2008, only 3 turned out to actually be related to terrorism.  Ironically, 65% of these 763 warrantless wiretaps were drug related.  The FEDS can now wiretap anyone without obtaining a warrant and use the defense of investigating potential terrorist activity.  There are no set guidelines whatsoever for identifying a suspected terrorist.  Always be brief, self-conscience and discreet on the phone.  Every computer has its own IP address and can be traced directly back to you.  Shred all incriminating documents or anything pertaining to your garden, i.e. grow shop receipts.


## POLICE QUESTIONING

There is a reality TV show on called, 48 Hours.  It follows homicide detectives as they try and solve a case.  It also shows extensively the tactics police use in questioning suspects.  They work in every way imaginable to deceive the suspect into incriminating themselves or confessing.  There are so many incidents where if the suspect would have just remained silent, they would have eventually walked.  Not that I condone murderers, but it is a real glimpse at how detectives work to manipulate a suspect.

Jail is a very scary place and it is very intimidating, but take a deep breath, if it's a state level marijuana bust and you are within your rights and the state's limits, it is very unlikely it will be pursued and the D.A. will likely drop the charges.  Call a family member or friend, get bailed out and have your attorney handle it.  Just keep your head under pressure, it's very intimidating and isolating, but don't answer questions and definitely do not sign anything without having a lawyer present.  Police may just be trying to question you to get more info on someone else.  Maybe the dispensary you work at, or your friend who's growing 50 plants and selling his crop to the dispensaries.  When the police tell you they have all the evidence they need to charge you, but want you to confess because they now care about you and it will make you look better to the judge, what they are really saying is we don't have enough evidence and we need you to confess so we can arrest you.


## MIRANDA WARNING

You have the right to remain silent
If you give up that right
Anything you say can and will be used against you in a court of law
You have the right to an attorney
If you cannot afford an attorney one will be provided by the court

We've all heard these words on our favorite police shows over and over again.  I think the biggest misconception is that police must read you these rights.  Not true!  The police do not have to read you your Miranda Rights.
Miranda only applies when there is

a. An interrogation

b. By a police officer

c. While you are still in police custody (keeping in mind that you do not have to be formally arrested to be in police custody)

Please know that you can invoke or re-invoke your right to remain silent at any time before or after police start questioning you.

## Search warrants

If the police come to your door with an arrest warrant, step outside and lock the door behind you.  Do not go back into the house.  Police can search any room that you go into.  If you slam the door in their face, they can use force to retrieve you, including breaking down the door.

Ask to see the warrant, a warrant must have a valid recent date, by recent within a couple weeks.  It must have the correct address, and a judge's signature.

## Marijuana and the IRS

For several years after states started passing medical marijuana laws, the IRS remained in the outfield. Technically the IRS is a federal agency and marijuana remains illegal under federal law. The IRS actually has a division called the, Illegal Source Financial Crimes Program which works to collect taxes on illegal income. But, many dispensaries were licensed through their state level government and were paying licensing fees and taxes at state level.

The golden model dispensary in this country since the early days of California decriminalization was Oakland based, Harborside. Harborside did business in a most professional and compliant manner. They did this to the point that they paid federal taxes. Last year, Harborside grossed a reported $22 Million Dollars in sales. They paid over $1.5 Million in taxes to the City of Oakland alone.

Over the past two years Harborside had been undergoing an IRS audit. Harborside maintains a practice of keeping perfectly clean and exact books. However, after months of patiently waiting on the outcome of the audit, Harborside was given a $2.5 Million Dollar bill from the IRS. Why? Under federal law business expenses for illegal businesses are non-deductible. Therefore, according to the IRS the only deduction that was allowed was the actual marijuana itself. All other operating expenses like rent, payroll, employee healthcare, everything was not deductible. Those expenses represent 40% of Harborside's gross revenue.

*§ 280E. Expenditures in connection with the illegal sale of drugs.*
*No deduction or credit shall be allowed for any amount paid or*
*incurred during the taxable year in carrying on any trade or*
*business if such trade or business (or the activities which comprise*
*such trade or business) consists of trafficking in controlled*
*substances (within the meaning of schedule I and II of the*
*Controlled Substances Act) which is prohibited by Federal law or*
*the law of any State in which such trade or business is conducted.*

At the time of this writing Harborside was preparing to appeal the decision, and should by rights be successful in taking the same deductions every other business is allowed.

Another situation arising in California at the time of this writing is the Feds demanding that California dispensaries close down within 45 days.  It appears that Obama has lied to all of us that he was not going to interfere with states decisions to allow medical marijuana. Meanwhile he cries about lack of funding, the economy continues to crash, and marijuana continues to have a potential to bring in a reported $1.7 Billion dollars annually according to Forbes.

Another scary recent development is the September, 2011 move by ATF. In a move that was nothing less than bold, the federal agency declared that medical marijuana patients could no longer possess firearms citing that they are prohibited because their marijuana use violates federal law. A recent ATF letter from the bureau's Assistant Director, Arthur Herbert advised gun dealers that if they knowingly sell a firearm to a medical marijuana patient that they could face strict enforcement through fines and other legal action.

A patient who now possesses a firearm is committing a felony under this new law.

At this time there are no cases in Colorado where anyone has been prosecuted for now illegally owning firearms. But this doesn't mean it won't come up down the line. The U.S. Attorney's office in Colorado has stated that the decision to prosecute would be determined on a case by case basis.

When purchasing a gun in Colorado, buyers are required to complete an ATF form which includes a question asking if the applicant is an unlawful user or addicted to drugs. Among those drugs listed is marijuana. Answer truthfully, and you will be denied buying the gun. Answer no and you have just committed a crime fairly similar in nature to illegally owning the gun.

# Growing Marijuana

Under federal law, growing marijuana is illegal and carries very serious consequences. However, under some states medical marijuana laws a patient and/or caregiver is allowed to collectively cultivate marijuana. The combined total number of plants that a patient and caregiver have when combined should never exceed 99 plants under any circumstance to avoid the threshold of serious federal consequence.

Basically speaking cannabis is a weed, and being a weed it is a fairly durable little plant. Therefore, many patients have elected to cultivate their own medicine to avoid the high prices of cannabis at dispensaries.

There are two general ways used to grow cannabis. The old traditional way using soil, or using a hydroponic grow system that uses water as the growing medium. Both ways are effective and a novice will find better success using the traditional soil technique or basic bubbler, drip ring, or Ebb Flow hydroponic technique .

A full grown mature marijuana plant can produce up to a pound to a pound and a half of smokable product. The going price for grams in dispensaries averages about $20. Multiply this by 12 plants and you are talking about a considerable amount of marijuana with a substantial value. But, a patient is not allowed to possess more than two and one half ounces of smokable cannabis at any one time.

Many patients sell these "overages" to dispensaries and other patients. So this option is an attractive alternative for many patients.

The time from planting to harvest is usually four months for indoor plants. During the vegetative stage of growing, the plant is kept under light anywhere from 16 to 24 hours. Once the plant reaches a mature size the light is reduced to 12 hours on, 12 hours off. This makes the plant believe that there is a change of season into fall and the plants starts it blooming stage. This is the stage where the plant actually produces buds. Once a plant starts it budding stage it usually takes about eight weeks till it is ready to be harvested. Harvesting early can leave you with buds that are not near their potential potency.

Things such as nutrients and PH also play an important part in successful cultivation.

Proper lighting is also an important element in gardening success. There are many different lighting systems on the market. Pro growers use lights that are 1000 watts, and use elaborate high-tech systems utilizing carbon dioxide and air circulation devices costing great deals of money. Another new technology making its way into gardens are LED grow lights. There are models out there offering all kinds of different light spectrums to choose from.

I have found that a simple and effective system can be set up for under $200. Sun Systems makes a 150W self-contained grow light system that retails for around a hundred bucks. Hydroponics stores sell 3 gallon buckets and three gallon lids that feature a mesh pot. The pot is filled with a growing medium like coco or perlite which surrounds the young plant.

A standard aquarium air hose is hooked up to a cheap aquarium air pump and ran through a hole drilled through the lid and connected to an air stone submerged in the water/nutrient solution in the bucket. The air stone allows adequate oxygen to remain in the water and reach the roots.

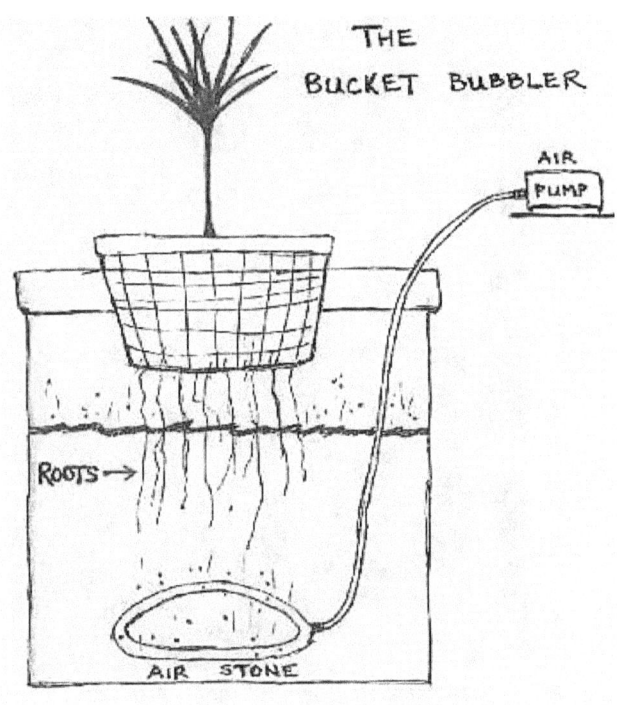

THE BUCKET BUBBLER

Drawing courtesy of Hydroponics Simplified

This is the most basic hydroponic system, referred to as a "bubbler" system. There are many different hydroponic systems out there and some get very elaborate and expensive, I have found the bubbler system combined with proper nutrients and adequate lighting to be very effective and also very cost effective. The 150 watt bulb even when on almost full time during the plants vegetative stage still is cost effective running an additional $16-$18/month to your power bill.

A marijuana garden grown utilizing a grow tent and soil

Outdoor gardening relies on natural sunlight and seasonal changes and is another ballpark altogether. Outdoor gardens are often the victim of attacks by spider mites and other plant pests. Outdoor gardens are also at risk of being spotted from above by helicopter or even nosey neighbors. Outdoor plants generally tend to grow taller and can literally reach above 12 feet in height on some strains. Because you cannot control the natural light of the sun, outdoor plants usually do not begin to bloom until fall when the daylight gets shorter.

**ALWAYS display your paperwork within your garden to show that your garden is medical and legal under state law.**

**There are many great grow books out there to use as a reference.**

There is a reason why I called Silver Surfer when I started writing my very first medical marijuana handbook and Silver Surfer has been the official vaporizer of every medical marijuana handbook since.

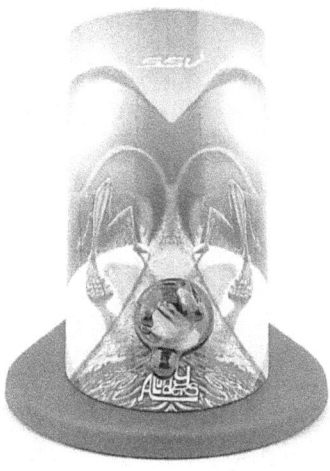

In my opinion, Silver Surfer Vaps are the finest vaporizers in the world.

As always we are proud to have them as the official vaporizer of their very own state's medical marijuana handbook.

### Silver Surfer Vaps
Made Here In Colorado
The official vaporizer of the Colorado Medical Marijuana Handbook and Colorado Marijuana Connoisseurs Handbook.

- Michael Malott
Author

## Marijuana Users as Parents

In the Medical Marihuana laws of most if not all states, parents are protected from unjust persecution because they are patients and parents.

Child Protective Services or Department of Family and Child Services are state agencies and therefore should follow state law.  However, sadly enough there are already documented cases on record where Child Protective Series (CPS) and Department of Family & Child Services (DFACS) have blatantly ignored the law and interfered with custody of the children of medical marijuana patients.  On the opposite end of this, I know people who run dispensaries, have children in school, and coach the team at their kid's school and have had no negative interaction with CPS or the parents of other children.  Of course, there are doctors in other states who have actually treated and continue to treat minors with great success using medical marijuana.

These agencies have relied on claims such as; children are being exposed to marijuana in the home.  They have made claims that a parent growing marijuana in the basement is subjecting the home to a home invasion & robbery, which is considered putting the child at risk.

Agencies such as these should certainly be considered a serious and ongoing threat to both recreational users and medical marijuana patients who are parents. This threat must be taken with absolute seriousness.

IF CPS or DFACS SHOWS UP AT YOUR DOOR
DO NOT ALLOW THEM TO ENTER YOUR HOME. When they ask if you mind if they come in to talk with you, simply say YES, I MIND!
DO NOT OPENLY OFFER ANY INFORMATION, politely ask them to contact you by mail and close the door. You are completely within your full legal right to deny them entry to your home. They want to enter the home to search for evidence showing parental unfitness. Unless they have genuine reason to believe a child is at immediate, serious risk, they will simply leave. IMMEDIATELY CONTACT A LAWYER. It takes an allegation of child abuse to get them to open an investigation and come to your home. When dealing with something as serious as this, have an attorney work as the liaison between you and CPS. Your attorney will generally arrange a meeting to take place, usually at the attorney's office where the CPS/DFACS investigator will interview you regarding the allegations. They also will have some contact with the child in most cases. Usually the case will be closed after that as unsubstantiated. You have no legal obligation to admit or deny your use of medical marijuana. CPS/DFACS will take a stance if you do declare medical marijuana use as to whether such use puts your child at risk, exposes that child to your medicating, or puts the child in any other form of endangerment. Like I mentioned prior, there is a case in Michigan where CPS claimed that one parent growing medical marijuana in their basement made that home a target to home invasion and therefore an unsafe location in their eyes for the child.

The ACLU has stepped in a couple times and they successfully forced these agencies to back off some parents who were properly registered medical marijuana patients. Some CPS/DFACS  social workers recognize the states laws or are just liberal, recognizing that marijuana isn't a threat. Others may in fact be patients themselves?

A safe practice using common sense is not to medicate anywhere around children.  (*Vaporizers are a good alternative*)

Do not leave cannabis or cannabis infused products anywhere where young children could access them. Remember medicated edibles will look very attractive to unsuspecting children.

Keep your plants away from children's access, your 14 year-old son may think showing your plants to his school buddies will impress them, but when those kids all tell their parents about your closet crop, it could cause problems.

The general rule of thumb here is to use common sense. There is no reason to advertise your medical marijuana use. If you are concerned, then be discreet.  The less people who know about it, the less the risk.

## How is marijuana benefiting people with HIV/AIDS?

Medical marijuana is commonly used to relieve nausea, vomiting, and appetite loss sometimes caused by HIV infection or by the medications used to treat HIV. Research has consistently found that these side effects are the leading reason patients interrupt or discontinue antiretroviral therapy (ART). Additionally, marijuana is sometimes used to relieve the pain of peripheral neuropathy, a condition which eventually impacts up to one-third of people with HIV.

Has medical marijuana been studied in HIV/AIDS patients? Yes. Although foot-dragging by federal authorities delayed needed research for years, two clinical trials have been completed and more are underway. Other information is available from observational studies. Results thus far have been consistently positive. A landmark study conducted at San Francisco General Hospital looked at the safety of medical marijuana use by patients on stable ART regimens and showed no adverse effects on viral load, CD4, or CD8 count, while the patients using marijuana gained more weight than those receiving a placebo.1 An observational study published in January 2005 found that patients experiencing ART-related nausea adhered to their drug regimens more consistently if they used marijuana. A study published in the journal *Neurology* in February 2007 reported that smoked marijuana "effectively relieved chronic pain from HIV-associated sensory neuropathy," with few side effects.

I've heard that marijuana may be harmful to the immune system.

Is this a danger to people with HIV/AIDS?
Such claims are based on test tube studies, often using enormous doses, rather than on studies of actual patients. In the San Francisco General Hospital study described above, patients using medical marijuana not only showed no signs of immunological damage, they actually gained more CD4 and CD8 cells than those receiving a placebo.

What do leading HIV/AIDS experts say about medical marijuana?
Leading HIV/AIDS organizations overwhelmingly believe seriously ill patients should be allowed to use medical marijuana without fear of arrest. The American Academy of HIV Medicine has stated, "When appropriately prescribed and monitored, marijuana/cannabis can provide immeasurable benefits for the health and well-being of our patients." Other supportive organizations include AIDS Action, Gay Men's Health Crisis, National Association of People With AIDS, AIDS Project Los Angeles, AIDS Foundation of Chicago, Test Positive Aware Network, AIDS Project Rhode Island, the New York State AIDS Advisory Council, Project Inform, San Francisco AIDS Foundation, and many others.

Do other medical and public health experts agree?
Yes. In a 1999 report commissioned by the White House, the National Academy of Sciences' Institute of Medicine wrote, "Nausea, appetite loss, pain, and anxiety are all afflictions of wasting and all can be mitigated by marijuana." The American College of Physicians, American Public Health Association, American Nurses Association and the state medical societies of New York, California, and Rhode Island are just a few of many medical organizations supporting legal access to medical marijuana. Prominent individuals supporting medical marijuana

access include former U.S. Surgeon General Dr. Joycelyn Elders, San Francisco Director of Health Dr. Mitch Katz, and Dr. Kenneth Mayer, director of Brown University's AIDS program.

What is the legal status of medical marijuana?

Fifteen states—Alaska, Arizona, California, Colorado, Hawaii, Maine, Michigan, Montana, Nevada, New Jersey, New Mexico, Oregon, Rhode Island, Vermont, and Washington, as well as the District of Columbia—permit medical use of marijuana if certain legal requirements followed. Unfortunately, federal law still classifies marijuana as having no medical use and as being too dangerous to use even under medical supervision—the same category as PCP and heroin. This is unscientific and harmful to people with HIV/AIDS and other serious illnesses.

Two true marijuana heroes; Jack Herer (l) and Dennis Peron (r)

# THE FDA & MARIJUANA FOR MEDICAL USE

The Food and Drug Administration (FDA) accepts or rejects a drug for medical use after receiving an application for a drug's approval as a prescription medicine, accompanied by supporting data provided by the company seeking to market that drug.

The FDA has never received such an application for marijuana. However, on April 20, 2006, the FDA issued an unusual press release restating the federal government's position that marijuana has not been shown to be a safe and effective medicine.

*Did the FDA study marijuana prior to issuing the statement?*
No. The FDA does not conduct its own trials of drugs, including marijuana. And the FDA statement did not refer to any new research or even any new review or analysis of existing data, even
though much new research was available.

*Did the FDA consider expert reviews of medical marijuana, such as the 1999 Institute of Medicine (IOM) report, which stated, "Nausea, appetite loss, pain and anxiety ... all can be mitigated by marijuana?"*
Apparently not. There is no mention of the IOM report in the FDA statement, and IOM report
co-author Dr. John Benson told *The New York Times* that the government "loves to ignore our report ... They would rather it never happened."

*So if the FDA didn't study marijuana or even review old data, why did it issue a statement at that particular time?*
The agency has never explained this, but the evidence points to political pressure. Congressman Mark Souder (R-IN), perhaps the most vehement opponent of medical marijuana in the U.S. Congress, wrote repeatedly to acting FDA Commissioner Andrew C. von Eschenbach seeking such a statement, writing in one

letter, "I am exasperated at FDA's failure to act against the fraudulent claims of 'medical' marijuana."

*Why haven't medical marijuana supporters tried to take marijuana through the FDA approval process?*

A group of researchers at the University of Massachusetts at Amherst is actively seeking to do this, but the Drug Enforcement Administration is blocking their efforts. The researchers are trying to create a facility to grow specific marijuana strains under controlled, reproducible conditions to test marijuana's efficacy for various indications. Such research is essential for FDA approval, but the DEA has refused to approve such a facility. Until this changes, the door to the FDA is blocked.

*Has any notable medical marijuana research occurred since the FDA statement?*

Yes. Among others, a University of California study found that marijuana effectively relieves peripheral neuropathy, a type of debilitating nerve pain that afflicts many patients with HIV/AIDS, with few side effects. And an observational study found that patients being treated for the deadly hepatitis C virus (HCV) were much more likely to be cured of the lethal virus if they used marijuana, apparently because marijuana relieves the side effects of harsh, anti-HCV drugs, allowing more patients to complete treatment.

*The FDA statement repeatedly refers to "smoked marijuana." Does this mean that other ways of administering marijuana might be okay?*

It should, but the statement's intent in this regard is unclear. Smoking has distinct advantages, such as rapid onset of action and ease of dose adjustment, but it also has known health risks. The FDA statement did not acknowledge such established non-smoked ways of using medical marijuana as teas, tinctures, and cooking marijuana in food. Of critical importance, several studies have shown that vaporization allows the use of whole marijuana with the advantages of smoking but few, if any, of the pulmonary risks associated with smoking. MPP is unaware of any statement from any federal government agency even acknowledging that this technology exists.

According to the groundbreaking medical report *Death by Medicine*, by Drs. Gary Null, Carolyn Dean, Martin Feldman, Debora Rasio and Dorothy Smith, 106,000 people in the United States die every year from conventional prescription drugs. Many have estimated the number to be more around 200,000, a year because of underreported cases of adverse drug reactions.

Compare this annual number to the all-time number of ZERO deaths associated with marijuana.

# Marijuana & the workplace

Many states laws do not contain any language pertaining to patient-employee relations or use of recreational or medical marijuana by employees. There is no protection afforded in the act which protects patients from being discharged for marijuana use or positive drug test results by their employers.

An employer by right can subject any employee to standard or random drug screening, and despite a patient's use of marijuana under the protection of that state's law that patient's employment can be terminated for failing a drug screening without any legal recourse against that employer.

However more and more employers are accepting both medical marijuana use and now recreational use by their employees under the act as long as it does not interfere with that employee's ability to safely and effectively perform their job. After all what a person does outside of work is really of no business to their employer. Some employers have even designed "medicating areas" at the workplace in a handful of instances for state approved patients to medicate.

While Colorado's Medical Marijuana Amendment specifically provides, in part, that "Nothing in this section shall require any employer to accommodate the medical use of marijuana in a workplace" it may very well conflict with Colorado's Unlawful Prohibition of Legal Activities as a Condition of Employment statute ("Lawful Off-Duty Activities Statute"), C.R.S. § 24-34-402.5. This Statute prevents an employer from terminating the employment of an employee due to the employee's engaging in any lawful activity off the premises of the employer during nonworking hours. The Statute creates exceptions when the termination: (1) relates to a bona fide occupational requirement or is reasonably and rationally related to the employment activities and responsibilities of a particular employee or a particular group of employees, rather than to all employees of the employer; (2) or it is necessary to avoid a conflict of interest with any responsibilities to the employer or the appearance of a conflict of interest.

The best policy to follow is to take a *"don't ask, don't tell"* attitude. Colorado's marijuana laws do not require an employer to accommodate the medical or recreational use of marijuana in the workplace. However, an employee can claim they only use marijuana off the job at home. If the employer then fires the employee for their marijuana use, the employee could then claim that the employer is violating Colorado's Lawful Off Duty Activities Statute. Generally the best direction is to keep it confidential and realize that your job doesn't need to know what you do outside of your job and you don't need to be advertising your great buds in your pocket. Bragging to the wrong co-workers will quickly backfire and could cost you your job. Simply, until provisions are introduced to your state's laws protecting everyone in the workplace, use common sense and discretion.

## Marijuana Use – nursing homes, assisted living facilities

Many state's laws also do not contain any language which permits or prohibits the use of medical marijuana by patients at these facilities. Check with the individual facility as to prohibitions regarding medical and recreational use of cannabis.

Edibles, tinctures, and vaporizers are all alternatives which are usually tolerated, although smoking of marijuana in these facilities may be strictly prohibited.

I have even found that some VA hospitals are actually accommodating medical marijuana use, including smoking for paraplegics and quadriplegic patients despite the VA's federal standing.

# MEDICAL MARIJUANA LAW
# The Colorado Constitution
# Article XVIII, Section 14

0-4-287 - ARTICLE XVIII - Miscellaneous Art. XVIII - Miscellaneous
0-4-287 - ARTICLE XVIII - Miscellaneous Art. XVIII - Miscellaneous

Section 14. Medical use of marijuana for persons suffering from debilitating medical conditions. (1) As used in this section, these terms are defined as follows:

(a) "Debilitating medical condition" means:

(I) Cancer, glaucoma, positive status for human immunodeficiency virus, or acquired immune deficiency syndrome, or treatment for such conditions;

(II) A chronic or debilitating disease or medical condition, or treatment for such conditions, which produces, for a specific patient, one or more of the following, and for which, in the professional opinion of the patient's physician, such condition or conditions reasonably may be alleviated by the medical use of marijuana: cachexia; severe pain; severe nausea; seizures, including those that are characteristic of epilepsy; or persistent muscle spasms, including those that are characteristic of multiple sclerosis; or

(III) Any other medical condition, or treatment for such condition, approved by the state health agency, pursuant to its rule making authority or its approval of any petition submitted by a patient or physician as provided in this section.

(b) "Medical use" means the acquisition, possession, production, use, or transportation of marijuana or paraphernalia related to the administration of such marijuana to address the symptoms or effects of a patient's debilitating medical condition, which may be authorized only after a diagnosis of the patient's debilitating medical condition by a physician or physicians, as provided by this section.

(c) "Parent" means a custodial mother or father of a patient under the age of eighteen years, any person having custody of a patient under the age of eighteen years, or any person serving as a legal guardian for a patient under the age of eighteen years.

(d) "Patient" means a person who has a debilitating medical condition.

(e) "Physician" means a doctor of medicine who maintains, in good standing, a license to practice medicine issued by the state of Colorado.

(f) "Primary care-giver" means a person, other than the patient and the patient's physician, who is eighteen years of age or older and has significant responsibility for managing the well-being of a patient who has a debilitating medical condition.

(g) "Registry identification card" means that document, issued by the state health agency, which identifies a patient authorized to engage in the medical use of marijuana and such patient's primary care-giver, if any has been designated.

(h) "State health agency" means that public health related entity of state government designated by the governor to establish and maintain a confidential registry of patients authorized to engage in the medical use of marijuana and enact rules to administer this program.

(i) "Usable form of marijuana" means the seeds, leaves, buds, and flowers of the plant (genus) cannabis, and any mixture or preparation thereof, which are appropriate for medical use as provided in this section, but excludes the plant's stalks, stems, and roots.

(j) "Written documentation" means a statement signed by a patient's physician or copies of the patient's pertinent medical records.

(2) (a) Except as otherwise provided in subsections (5), (6), and (8) of this section, a patient or primary care-giver charged with a violation of the state's criminal laws related to the patient's medical use of marijuana will be deemed to have established an affirmative defense to such allegation where:

(I) The patient was previously diagnosed by a physician as having a debilitating medical condition;

(II) The patient was advised by his or her physician, in the context of a bona fide physician-patient relationship, that the patient might benefit from the medical use of marijuana in connection with a debilitating medical condition; and

(III) The patient and his or her primary care-giver were collectively in possession of amounts of marijuana only as permitted under this section.

This affirmative defense shall not exclude the assertion of any other defense where a patient or primary care-giver is charged with a violation of state law related to the patient's medical use of marijuana.

(b) Effective June 1, 2001, it shall be an exception from the state's criminal laws for any patient or primary care-giver in lawful possession of a registry identification card to engage or assist in the medical use of marijuana, except as otherwise provided in subsections (5) and (8) of this section.

(c) It shall be an exception from the state's criminal laws for any physician to:

(I) Advise a patient whom the physician has diagnosed as having a debilitating medical condition, about the risks and benefits of medical use of marijuana or that he or she might benefit from the medical use of marijuana, provided that such advice is based upon the physician's contemporaneous assessment of the patient's medical history and current medical condition and a bona fide physician-patient relationship; or

(II) Provide a patient with written documentation, based upon the physician's contemporaneous assessment of the patient's medical history and current medical condition and a bona fide physician-patient relationship, stating that the patient has a debilitating medical condition and might benefit from the medical use of marijuana.

No physician shall be denied any rights or privileges for the acts authorized by this subsection.

(d) Notwithstanding the foregoing provisions, no person, including a patient or primary care-giver, shall be entitled to the protection of this section for his or her acquisition, possession, manufacture, production, use, sale, distribution, dispensing, or transportation of marijuana for any use other than medical use.

(e) Any property interest that is possessed, owned, or used in connection with the medical use of marijuana or acts incidental to such use, shall not be harmed, neglected, injured, or destroyed while in the possession of state or local law enforcement officials where such property has been seized in connection with the claimed medical use of marijuana. Any such property interest shall not be forfeited under any provision of state law providing for the forfeiture of property other than as a sentence imposed after conviction of a criminal offense or entry of a plea of guilty to such offense. Marijuana and paraphernalia seized by state or local law enforcement officials from a patient or primary care-giver in connection with the claimed medical use of marijuana shall be returned immediately upon the determination of the district attorney or his or her designee that the patient or primary care-giver is entitled to the protection contained in this section as may be evidenced, for example, by a decision not to prosecute, the dismissal of charges, or acquittal.

(3) The state health agency shall create and maintain a confidential registry of patients who have applied for and are entitled to receive a registry identification card according to the criteria set forth in this subsection, effective June 1, 2001.

(a) No person shall be permitted to gain access to any information about patients in the state health agency's confidential registry, or any information otherwise maintained by the state health agency about physicians and primary care-givers, except for authorized employees of the state health agency in the course of their official duties and authorized employees of state or local law enforcement agencies which have stopped or arrested a person who claims to be engaged in the medical use of marijuana and in possession of a registry identification card or its functional equivalent, pursuant to paragraph (e) of this subsection (3). Authorized employees of state or local law enforcement agencies shall be granted access to the information contained within the state health agency's confidential registry only for the purpose of verifying that an individual who has presented a registry identification card to a state or local law enforcement official is lawfully in possession of such card.

(b) In order to be placed on the state's confidential registry for the medical use of marijuana, a patient must reside in Colorado and submit the completed application form adopted by the state health agency, including the following information, to the state health agency:

(I) The original or a copy of written documentation stating that the patient has been diagnosed with a debilitating medical condition and the physician's conclusion that the patient might benefit from the medical use of marijuana;

(II) The name, address, date of birth, and social security number of the patient;

(III) The name, address, and telephone number of the patient's physician; and

(IV) The name and address of the patient's primary care-giver, if one is designated at the time of application.

(c) Within thirty days of receiving the information referred to in subparagraphs (3) (b) (I)-(IV), the state health agency shall verify medical information contained in the patient's written documentation. The agency shall notify the applicant that his or her application for a registry identification card has been denied if the agency's review of such documentation discloses that: the information required pursuant to paragraph (3) (b) of this section has not been provided or has been falsified; the documentation fails to state that the patient has a debilitating medical condition specified in this section or by state health agency rule; or the physician does not have a license to practice medicine issued by the state of Colorado. Otherwise, not more than five days after verifying such information, the state health agency shall issue one serially numbered registry identification card to the patient, stating:

(I) The patient's name, address, date of birth, and social security number;

(II) That the patient's name has been certified to the state health agency as a person who has a debilitating medical condition, whereby the patient may address such condition with the medical use of marijuana;

(III) The date of issuance of the registry identification card and the date of expiration of such card, which shall be one year from the date of issuance; and

(IV) The name and address of the patient's primary care-giver, if any is designated at the time of application.

(d) Except for patients applying pursuant to subsection (6) of this section, where the state health agency, within thirty-five days of receipt of an application, fails to issue a registry identification card or fails to issue verbal or written notice of denial of such application, the patient's application for such card will be deemed to have been approved. Receipt shall be deemed to have occurred upon delivery to the state health agency, or deposit in the United States mails. Notwithstanding the foregoing, no application shall be deemed received prior to June 1, 1999. A patient who is questioned by any state or local law enforcement official about his or her medical use of marijuana shall provide a copy of the application submitted to the state health agency, including the written documentation and proof of the date of mailing or other transmission of the written documentation for delivery to the state health agency, which shall be accorded the same legal effect as a registry identification card, until such time as the patient receives notice that the application has been denied.

(e) A patient whose application has been denied by the state health agency may not reapply during the six months following the date of the denial and may not use an application for a registry identification card as provided in paragraph (3) (d) of this section. The denial of a registry identification card shall be considered a final agency action. Only the patient whose application has been denied shall have standing to contest the agency action.

(f) When there has been a change in the name, address, physician, or primary care- giver of a patient who has qualified for a registry identification card, that patient must notify the state health agency of any such change within ten days. A patient who has not designated a primary care-giver at the time of application to the state health agency may do so in writing at any time during the effective period of the registry identification card, and the primary care-giver may act in this capacity after such designation. To maintain an effective registry identification card, a patient must annually resubmit, at least thirty days prior to the expiration date stated on the registry identification card, updated written documentation to the state health agency, as well as the name and address of the patient's primary care-giver, if any is designated at such time.

(g) Authorized employees of state or local law enforcement agencies shall immediately notify the state health agency when any person in possession of a registry identification card has been determined by a court of law to have willfully violated the provisions of this section or its implementing legislation, or has pled guilty to such offense.

(h) A patient who no longer has a debilitating medical condition shall return his or her registry identification card to the state health agency within twenty-four hours of receiving such diagnosis by his or her physician.

(i) The state health agency may determine and levy reasonable fees to pay for any direct or indirect administrative costs associated with its role in this program.

(4) (a) A patient may engage in the medical use of marijuana, with no more marijuana than is medically necessary to address a debilitating medical condition. A patient's medical use of marijuana, within the following limits, is lawful:

(I) No more than two ounces of a usable form of marijuana; and

(II) No more than six marijuana plants, with three or fewer being mature, flowering plants that are producing a usable form of marijuana.

(b) For quantities of marijuana in excess of these amounts, a patient or his or her primary care-giver may raise as an affirmative defense to charges of violation of state law that such greater amounts were medically necessary to address the patient's debilitating medical condition.

(5) (a) No patient shall:

(I) Engage in the medical use of marijuana in a way that endangers the health or well-being of any person; or

(II) Engage in the medical use of marijuana in plain view of, or in a place open to, the general public.

(b) In addition to any other penalties provided by law, the state health agency shall revoke for a period of one year the registry identification card of any patient found to have willfully violated the provisions of this section or the implementing legislation adopted by the general assembly.

(6) Notwithstanding paragraphs (2) (a) and (3) (d) of this section, no patient under eighteen years of age shall engage in the medical use of marijuana unless:

(a) Two physicians have diagnosed the patient as having a debilitating medical condition;

(b) One of the physicians referred to in paragraph (6) (a) has explained the possible risks and benefits of medical use of marijuana to the patient and each of the patient's parents residing in Colorado;

(c) The physicians referred to in paragraph (6) (b) has provided the patient with the written documentation, specified in subparagraph (3) (b) (I);

(d) Each of the patient's parents residing in Colorado consent in writing to the state health agency to permit the patient to engage in the medical use of marijuana;

(e) A parent residing in Colorado consents in writing to serve as a patient's primary care-giver;

(f) A parent serving as a primary care-giver completes and submits an application for a registry identification card as provided in subparagraph (3) (b) of this section and the written consents referred to in paragraph (6) (d) to the state health agency;

(g) The state health agency approves the patient's application and transmits the patient's registry identification card to the parent designated as a primary care-giver;

(h) The patient and primary care-giver collectively possess amounts of marijuana no greater than those specified in subparagraph (4) (a) (I) and (II); and

(i) The primary care-giver controls the acquisition of such marijuana and the dosage and frequency of its use by the patient.

(7) Not later than March 1, 2001, the governor shall designate, by executive order, the state health agency as defined in paragraph (1) (g) of this section.

(8) Not later than April 30, 2001, the General Assembly shall define such terms and enact such legislation as may be necessary for implementation of this section, as well as determine and enact criminal penalties for:

(a) Fraudulent representation of a medical condition by a patient to a physician, state health agency, or state or local law enforcement official for the purpose of falsely obtaining a registry identification card or avoiding arrest and prosecution;

(b) Fraudulent use or theft of any person's registry identification card to acquire, possess, produce, use, sell, distribute, or transport marijuana, including but not limited to cards that are required to be returned where patients are no longer diagnosed as having a debilitating medical condition;

(c) Fraudulent production or counterfeiting of, or tampering with, one or more registry identification cards; or

(d) Breach of confidentiality of information provided to or by the state health agency.

(9) Not later than June 1, 2001, the state health agency shall develop and make available to residents of Colorado an application form for persons seeking to be listed on the confidential registry of patients. By such date, the state health agency shall also enact rules of administration, including but not limited to rules governing the establishment and confidentiality of the registry, the verification of medical information, the issuance and form of registry identification cards, communications with law enforcement officials about registry identification cards that have been suspended where a patient is no longer diagnosed as having a debilitating medical condition, and the manner in which the agency may consider adding debilitating medical conditions to the list provided in this section. Beginning June 1, 2001, the state health agency shall accept physician or patient initiated petitions to add debilitating medical conditions to the list provided in this section and, after such hearing as the state health agency deems appropriate, shall approve or deny such petitions within one hundred eighty days of submission. The decision to approve or deny a petition shall be considered a final agency action.

(10) (a) No governmental, private, or any other health insurance provider shall be required to be liable for any claim for reimbursement for the medical use of marijuana.

(b) Nothing in this section shall require any employer to accommodate the medical use of marijuana in any work place.

(11) Unless otherwise provided by this section, all provisions of this section shall become effective upon official declaration of the vote hereon by proclamation of the governor, pursuant to article

V, section (1) (4), and shall apply to acts or offenses committed on or after that date.

Enacted by the People November 7, 2000 -- Effective upon proclamation of the Governor.

# YOU WANT CHANGE?

It's your responsibility to register to vote and make your voice heard

Objection: There is little trustworthy evidence that smoked marijuana actually works.

Reply: In a White House-commissioned 1999 report, the National Academy of Sciences' Institute of Medicine, in a review of the current science at the time, found extensive scientific evidence verifying that marijuana has medical value for patients suffering from pain, nausea, appetite loss, and other symptoms of illnesses such as cancer, multiple sclerosis, and HIV/AIDS. The IOM report stated, "Nausea, appetite loss, pain, and anxiety are all afflictions of wasting and all can be mitigated by marijuana ... there are patients with debilitating symptoms for whom smoked marijuana might provide relief." Subsequent studies since the 1999 Institute of Medicine report, including randomized, double-blind, placebo-controlled clinical trials, continue to show the therapeutic value of marijuana in treating a wide array of debilitating medical conditions, including relieving medication side effects and thus improving the likelihood that patients will adhere to life-prolonging treatments for HIV/AIDS and Hepatitis C. Marijuana was also shown to be effective at alleviating HIV/AIDS neuropathy, a painful condition for which there are no FDA-approved treatments. That is why, in January 2008, the American College of Physicians – the second-largest physician group in the country – called for marijuana to be reclassified under federal law to allow physician prescriptions, citing "marijuana's proven efficacy at treating certain symptoms and its relatively low toxicity."

Objection: Marijuana is an addictive drug that poses significant health consequences to its users.

Reply: Marijuana and cannabinoids have a generally excellent safety profile. Unlike many medicines, acute lethal overdoses of marijuana have not been reported, and research has not documented increased mortality attributable to chronic use. Concerns about immunological impairment have not been borne out in research with AIDS patients. No medications are without risk; however, medical marijuana is relatively benign compared to many routinely prescribed drugs. The American College of Physicians noted marijuana's "relatively low toxicity" in its January 2008 statement. Further, the American Public Health Association's official position statement on medical marijuana states, "[M]arijuana has an extremely wide acute margin of safety for use under physician supervision and cannot cause lethal reactions ... greater harm is caused by the legal consequences of its prohibition than possible risks of medicinal use." And, in its 1999 study, the Institute of Medicine concluded that "Compared to most other drugs ... dependence among marijuana users is relatively rare."

Objection: Smoked marijuana is a known carcinogen with hundreds of well- documented negative effects.

Reply: In fact, the largest and most well-controlled studies have consistently found that marijuana smokers don't have higher rates of lung cancer or other typically tobacco-related cancers. A 2006 NIDA-funded case-control study co- authored by Dr. Donald Tashkin — one of the world's foremost experts on the respiratory effects of illicit drugs — found no increased risk of lung cancer among even the heaviest marijuana smokers. Indeed, there was a trend toward lower lung cancer risk among even heavy marijuana smokers as compared to non-smokers, though the difference did not reach statistical significance. One possible explanation for this is the growing body of evidence documenting the anti-tumor actions of cannabinoids. Also, a 1997 Kaiser Permanente epidemiological study of 65,000 subjects showed no increase in lung or other tobacco-related cancers due to marijuana smoking, suggesting the potential of a favorable risk/benefit ratio for smoked medical marijuana in some chronic and/or painful conditions. It is worth noting in this context that the phrase "smoked marijuana" is a red herring. Marijuana need not be administered by smoking: It can be taken in food, tea, or through a smokeless vaporizer. Vaporization technology, discussed in the American College of Physicians' position paper, has been shown to achieve the drug delivery benefits of inhalation — rapid action and ease of dose titration — without the harmful combustion products contained in smoke.

Objection: Marijuana can cause schizophrenia.

Reply: Concerns have been raised in recent years regarding associations between marijuana use and acute psychosis and schizophrenia. While marijuana users have higher rates of psychotic symptoms or diagnosed psychosis than non-users, the relative risk remains modest, and increased rates of marijuana use in the U.S. and Australia during the 1970s and 1980s did not lead to increased incidence of schizophrenia. Overall, the evidence suggests that marijuana use can precipitate psychosis in vulnerable individuals but is unlikely to cause the illness in otherwise normal persons. Use of cannabinoids in patients with a family or personal history of psychosis should generally be avoided until more is known.

DOCTORS AND PATIENTS:

Objection: The mere existence of medical marijuana access laws puts both patient and physician in harm's way.

Reply: Medical marijuana access promotes physician autonomy to recommend the evidence-based medical treatment that is best for a patient, without legal punishment. Organized medicine should recognize the difference between licensing a drug for marketing and simply exempting patients using marijuana in state-sanctioned programs under the advice and supervision of a physician from criminal prosecution. Federal courts have upheld the right of physicians to recommend marijuana to patients, and physicians in the 13 medical marijuana states who follow appropriate standards of care when recommending marijuana have not experienced difficulties.

Objection: There is no clear reason why the American Medical Association and other physician groups should support patient protection for legitimate medical marijuana users in the 13 state-sanctioned programs.

Reply: Existing AMA policy already affirms the protection of physicians practicing in medical marijuana states from federal prosecution for discussing and recommending medical marijuana to their patients. It does not, however, extend protection to the patients themselves in medical marijuana states, an important omission that warrants addressing by the AMA. In addition to arrest, fines, and confiscation of property and legally obtained supplies of medical marijuana, patients and their families have been subjected to DEA "SWAT team" style invasions of their homes and the sudden discontinuation of their medical marijuana treatment. This can lead to exacerbation of chronic pain, wasting, and other serious medical conditions previously controlled by medical marijuana. Subjecting seriously ill patients to arrest and prosecution constitutes cruel and unusual punishment, which is why the editor-in-chief of the *New England Journal of Medicine* called the federal ban on the medical use of

marijuana "misguided, heavy-handed, and inhumane." Federal law makes no distinction between those who possess or grow marijuana for medical purposes and those who are using it recreationally: the same penalties apply. The possession of a single marijuana cigarette can result in a sentence of up to one year, while the cultivation of a single marijuana plant can produce a sentence of up to five years.
[http://www.justice.gov/dea/agency/penalties.htm]

Objection: We don't know what the general physician sentiment on this issue is.

Reply: In a 2005 poll conducted by HCD Research and the Muhlenberg College Institute of Public Opinion of 922 U.S. office-based physicians weighted by specialty and geography, 74% disagreed that "the federal government should be able to prosecute those who use, grow, or obtain marijuana prescribed or recommended by their doctor for chronic pain within the guidelines of state law."

Objection: Supporting any form of medical marijuana access is politically risky for physician organizations.

Reply: Across the country and with increasing frequency, public opinion polls — and actual votes at the ballot box — show that support for medical marijuana is overwhelming, steadily rising, and cuts across demographic and party lines. A 2004 AARP poll showed that 72% of seniors support medical marijuana, and a 2005 Gallup poll found that 78% of Americans support "making marijuana legally available for doctors to prescribe in order to reduce pain and suffering." Not one of the state medical marijuana laws passed since 1996 has been repealed. Indeed, when legislatures have made changes to these laws, it has generally been to extend and expand them. For example, in 2002, Maine increased the amount of medical marijuana that patients are allowed to possess. In 2007, Vermont expanded the list of conditions covered under the program and increased the number of marijuana plants that patients could legally grow. These are not the sorts of actions that legislators take when a law is unpopular.

Objection: The American Medical Association is a leader in organized medicine and their policy on medical marijuana is clear, consistent, and sufficient at this time.

Reply: The Connecticut newspaper *Guilford Courier* interviewed AMA spokesperson Robert Mills (Office of Media Relations) and reported on July 15, 2005, that "the AMA recommends keeping marijuana [unchanged] as a controlled substance 'pending the outcomes of studies to prove the application and efficacy of marijuana and other related cannabinoids'" but, in contrast, Mills and an American Cancer Society spokesman "both mentioned that patients afflicted with cancer and other painful medical conditions should not be prosecuted for trying to alleviate their suffering." Furthermore, the AMA is a member organization of the Accreditation Council for Continuing Medical Education (ACCME). Medical colleges and hospitals accredited by the ACCME have awarded AMA PRA Category 1 Credits to physicians attending conferences and CME events focusing on medical marijuana clinical therapeutics and research. The AMA defines the content of CME as "the body of knowledge and skills generally recognized and accepted by the profession as within the basic medical sciences, the discipline of clinical medicine, and the provision of health care to the public."
Objection: Marijuana use can cause psychosis in some people and, if a patient who had a recommendation from a physician commits a violent act, that physician could be subject to criminal prosecution.

Reply: Thousands of physicians have recommended medical marijuana to tens of thousands of patients in the 13 states where it is sanctioned by law. There have been no recorded cases of a psychotic reaction by a patient to marijuana that have resulted in a physician being put at legal or criminal risk for issuing such a recommendation. A great many prescription medicines can cause adverse psychiatric reactions, some much more commonly than the putative link between marijuana and psychosis. This is the sort of risk that physicians manage every day by appropriately evaluating, screening, and monitoring patients.

Objection: If wider access were allowed to medical marijuana for legitimate patients, there would be an increase in the amount of marijuana-related car crashes and fatalities.

Reply: As with the use of any medication, common sense and personal responsibility must prevail. Literally hundreds of prescription and over-the- counter drugs — taken every day by millions of Americans — can cause drowsiness or slowed reactions and should not be used while driving. We do not deny patients who need these medicines the relief they need because driving while taking them is contraindicated; instead, we expect them to use common sense. Medical marijuana patients should be held accountable to the same standards and laws as those who take any medicine with the potential to impair coordination and decision-making. One-fifth of the U.S. population now lives in states with medical marijuana laws, but there is no published evidence indicating that the medical use of marijuana has led to an increase in motor vehicle accidents in any of these states.

Objection: Increased medical marijuana access would lead to decreases in workplace productivity.

Reply: There is no reason to believe that this is the case, and some reason to believe that the opposite is true. No medical marijuana law requires employers to accommodate marijuana use in the workplace. Many patients, however, report that marijuana, by providing improved relief of nausea, pain, loss of sleep, and other symptoms, allows them to work more productively than they could before beginning a medical marijuana regimen. And some have found that their marijuana regimen actually allowed them to return to work, when without using marijuana they had been too ill to do so.


## CHILDREN, GATEWAYS, AND DIVERSION:

Objection: Affirmative positions supporting medical marijuana endanger our children and encourage abuse of the drug.

Reply: Of the 13 medical marijuana states, 11 now have data on teen marijuana use from both before and after the medical marijuana laws were passed. Adolescent marijuana use has not risen in a single one of these states [http://www.mpp.org/assets/pdfs/general/TeenUseReport_0 608.pdf]. Instead, it has declined since medical marijuana became legal. For example, in California — the state where tales of abuse appear to be most common — the state-sponsored California Student Survey found that 34.2 percent of ninth graders reported having used marijuana in the past six months in 1995-96, the last survey before California's medical marijuana law, Proposition 215, passed. This represented a near-doubling from the 1991-92 survey. Teen marijuana use began to decline in the 1997-98 survey, the first conducted after Prop. 215 passed. By 1999-2000, past-six-months marijuana use by ninth graders had plunged to 19.2 percent, and it has declined even further since then.

[http://safestate.org/documents/CSS_11_Tables.pdf] The American College of Physicians notes, "Opiates are highly addictive yet medically effective substances and are classified as Schedule II substances," but "there is no evidence to suggest that medical use of opiates has increased perception that their illicit use is safe or acceptable."

Objection: Marijuana is a gateway drug to harder substances, and therefore medical marijuana use will lead to dangerous drug use.

Reply: In science, the distinction between correlation and causation is crucial. The "gateway theory" has been roundly debunked by many credible sources. According to a 2006 study commissioned by the British Parliament, "the gateway theory has little evidence to support it despite copious research." The Institute of Medicine has concluded, "There is no evidence that marijuana serves as a stepping stone [to other drugs] on the basis of its particular physiological effect." The American College of Physicians noted in February 2008, "Marijuana has not been proven to be the cause or even the most serious predictor of serious drug abuse. It is also important to note that the data on marijuana's role in illicit drug use progression only pertains to its non-medical use." In any case, it is absurd on its face to cite a supposed "gateway effect" for patients who are already routinely prescribed opiates and other highly addictive, potentially deadly narcotics. Medical marijuana is a safe alternative for patients whose other options are not as reliable or effective.

Objection: Medical marijuana laws create opportunities for diversion to illegal markets.

Reply: Recent press reports have indicated that the DEA is continuing to close down medical marijuana dispensaries ("buyers' clubs"). Reports emphasize the large volume of marijuana being cultivated by some dispensaries and the risk of diversion to illegal sales outside of the medical marijuana patient community. While these risks are not trivial, neither is the ongoing problem of diversion of prescription drugs to illicit uses— and yet we do not deny patients who need these drugs appropriate relief because of such abuse. The best way to ensure that medical marijuana is not diverted to illicit uses is through appropriate regulation and control, but federal law enforcement efforts have actually hampered and interfered with attempts by state and local governments to implement such controls. The AMA could encourage state and local governments to develop stronger systems of licensing and oversight of medical marijuana production. It could also call upon the federal government either to participate constructively in such regulation or get out of the way of state efforts to do so.


## DIFFICULTIES AND OBSTACLES OF DOING RESEARCH:

Objection: The American Medical Association and others already have pro- research positions on medical marijuana.

Reply: The current research climate for marijuana has created a significant chilling effect for researchers wanting to pursue FDA-approved clinical and basic research on the safety and efficacy of medical marijuana. While existing AMA policy recommends that NIDA should provide medical marijuana for all FDA-approved clinical and basic research studies in the U.S., this recommendation has gone unheeded by NIDA, which has refused to supply medical marijuana to several privately-funded, FDA-approved research projects and has delayed initiation of other projects (including those approved and funded by NIDA) for several years. A more strongly worded position that specifically recommends marijuana's reclassification under federal law and/or the licensing of private medical marijuana production facilities that meet all regulatory requirements to produce pharmaceutical- grade marijuana for use exclusively in federally-approved research would provide a solution to the current no-win situation. It is entirely appropriate for organized medicine to respond to the current legal limbo to help create a positive climate for increased research.

Objection: There have been many federally-sanctioned studies on the medical use of marijuana in the past decade. These studies are continuing today, and they will continue in the future.

Reply: On the contrary, only a handful of medical marijuana studies have been allowed to proceed, and only one is presently underway. These have been small pilot studies, and while they have been consistently successful, the federal government is actively obstructing the type of medical marijuana studies that would be needed to obtain FDA approval. Most notably, a group of researchers at the University of Massachusetts at Amherst has been seeking to conduct formal trials for years, but the Drug Enforcement Administration is blocking their efforts. The researchers are trying to create a facility to grow specific marijuana strains under controlled, reproducible conditions to test marijuana's efficacy for various indications. Such research is essential for FDA approval, but the DEA has refused to approve such a facility.

Objection: There haven't been any double-blind, placebo-controlled studies proving marijuana's effectiveness.

Reply: Despite the many difficulties in acquiring marijuana for research, in 2007, Dr. Donald Abrams of the University of California, San Francisco, published just such a study that found marijuana to be safe and effective at treating peripheral neuropathy, which causes great suffering to HIV/AIDS patients. There are no FDA-approved treatments for peripheral neuropathy, which is notoriously resistant to treatment with conventional pain medications. In the UCSF study, marijuana was clearly shown to give relief. In this randomized, double-blind, placebo-controlled trial, a majority of patients had a greater than 30 percent reduction in pain after smoking marijuana. In another randomized, double-blind, placebo-controlled study published in April 2008 by the *Journal of Pain*, marijuana was found to be effective at relieving neuropathic pain from a variety of causes, including diabetes, multiple sclerosis, and spinal injury.

Objection: There has been no research on non-smoked delivery systems for marijuana.

Reply: The IOM expressed concern about the health risks of smoking and urged development of a "nonsmoked, rapid-onset cannabinoid drug delivery system," but noted that in the meantime, "we acknowledge that there is no clear alternative for people suffering from chronic conditions that might be relieved by smoking marijuana, such as pain or AIDS wasting." The answer to the IOM's concerns about smoking is vaporizers, which take advantage of the fact that cannabinoids vaporize at a temperature well below that at which marijuana burns. Vaporizers allow patients to inhale cannabinoid vapors without smoking, achieving the same rapid action and easy dose titration without the tars and other irritants found in smoke. Several studies of such devices have now been published. In a study of one such device, the Volcano, researchers confirmed that the device works as intended, stating, "What is currently needed for optimal use of medicinal cannabinoids is a feasible, nonsmoked rapid-onset delivery system. With the Volcano, a safe and effective delivery system appears to be available to patients."

Objection: Sativex® will be approved soon.

Reply: Sativex® is a concentrated extract of the components of natural marijuana that has been developed for sublingual use to counter pain associated with advanced cancer and pain/spasticity associated with multiple sclerosis. An FDA-approved clinical study for advanced cancer pain is underway. Additional studies will likely be needed prior to approval by the FDA, making it likely that Sativex® would not be available in the U.S. for at least three more years. Meanwhile, many thousands of people are already obtaining significant symptom relief with medical marijuana in the 12 states with medical marijuana programs, but they are still subject to federal prosecution and intimidation. Sativex may well prove to be a useful product, but it has been shown to have drawbacks. It takes far longer to reach peak blood levels than inhaled marijuana, and the alcohol-based spray has been associated with oral lesions.

# What Leaders are saying about the medical use of marijuana

The following is a representative sample of the large number of government panels, medical organizations, health charities and individuals of note who have publicly stated their support for medical access to marijuana and/or their opposition to criminal penalties for medical marijuana users.

" Nausea, appetite loss, pain and anxiety are all afflictions of wasting, and all can be mitigated by marijuana."
— Institute of Medicine, "Marijuana and Medicine: Assessing the Science Base," 1999

" [T]here will likely always be a subpopulation of patients who do not respond well to other medications ... The critical issue is not whether marijuana or cannabinoid drugs might be superior to the new drugs, but whether some group of patients might obtain added or better relief from marijuana or cannabinoid drugs ... Although some medications are more effective than marijuana for these problems, they are not equally effective in all patients."
— Institute of Medicine, "Marijuana and Medicine: Assessing the Science Base," 1999"

ACP strongly urges protection from criminal or civil penalties for patients who use medical marijuana as permitted under state laws."

—American College of Physicians(representing 124,000 members, ACP is the largest specialty and second largest medical society in the U.S.),"Supporting Research into the Therapeutic Role of Marijuana,"February 2008

"Considering the evidence available today about the potential therapeutic benefits and risks associated with marijuana and its cannabinoids, ACP believes that it is time to review the evidence to determine whether reclassification is appropriate ... We believe that an evidence-based review by federal regulatory authorities on the safety and efficacy of marijuana and cannabinoids for therapeutic purposes will likely provide evidence to support both appropriate reclassification and adjustment of federal drug enforcement laws, reduce conflict between federal and state law, and strengthen public confidence in the federal regulatory structure."
—American College of Physicians(representing 124,000 members, ACP is the largest specialty and second largest medical society in the U.S.),"Supporting Research into the Therapeutic Role of Marijuana,An Addendum by the Health and Public Policy Committee," 2008

"[I]t is the responsibility of federal regulatory agencies to take the steps necessary to conduct an  evidence-based evaluation of the safety and effectiveness of marijuana and its cannabinoids for therapeutic purposes..."
—American College of Physicians(representing 124,000 members, ACP is the largestspecialty and second largest medical society in the U.S.),"Supporting Research into the Therapeutic Role of Marijuana,An Addendum by the Health and Public Policy Committee," 2008"

[T]he Leukemia & Lymphoma Society supports legislation to remove criminal and civil sanctions for the doctor-advised, medical use of marijuana by patients with serious physical medical conditions ... [the] Leukemia & Lymphoma Society strongly urge that in a state where patients are permitted to use marijuana medicinally for serious and/or chronic illnesses and a patient's physician has recommended its use in accordance with that state's law and that state's medical practice standards, the patient should not be subject to federal criminal penalties for such medical use."
— Leukemia & Lymphoma Society, July 2007

"The American Academy of Addiction Psychiatry endorses the Institute of Medicine (IOM) report supporting the therapeutic value of cannabinoid drugs for pain relief, control of nausea and vomiting and appetite stimulations for debilitating conditions such as AIDS. We are in favor of compassion for the ill and the availability of marijuana for medical purposes based on current evidence."
— American Academy of Addiction Psychiatry, "Medical Use of Marijuana," June 2002, www.aaap.org/policies/marijuana.html

"[We ask] that our AMA support reclassification of marijuana's status as a Schedule I controlled substance into a more appropriate schedule."
—Medical Student Section of the American Medical Association,Marijuana: Medical Use and Research, June 14, 2008"

[The AAFP accepts the use of medical marijuana] under medical supervision and control for specific medical indications."
— American Academy of Family Physicians, 1989, reaffirmed in 2001

" When appropriately prescribed and monitored, marijuana/cannabis can provide immeasurable benefits for the health and well-being of our patients."
— American Academy of HIV Medicine, 2003

" Therefore be it resolved that the American Nurses Association will: ... Support the right of patients to have safe access to therapeutic marijuana/cannabis under appropriate prescriber supervision."
— American Nurses Association, resolution, 2003

" The CMA has always recognized and acknowledged the unique requirements of those individuals suffering from a terminal illness or chronic disease for which conventional therapies have not been effective and for whom marijuana for medicinal purposes may provide relief."
— Canadian Medical Association, January 2006,

" Present evidence indicates that [cannabinoids] are remarkably safe drugs, with a side-effects profile superior to many drugs used for the same indications."
— British Medical Association, November 1997

" For a significant number of patients, clinical experience and research confirm that marijuana serves as the only effective medicine for relieving pain, suppressing nausea or stimulating appetite. Numerous studies by blue-ribbon government panels and federally funded, peer-reviewed scientific studies have consistently found that marijuana is effective for treating certain debilitating symptoms."
— American Pain Foundation, American Medical Women's Association, Lymphoma Foundation of America, American Nurses Association, California Nurses Association, AIDS Action Council,

National Women's Health Network, Doctors of the World-USA, Gay Men's Health Crisis, Amici Curiae in Support of Petitioner, *Ross v. Ragingwire*, 2006 WL 3244938 (August 7, 2006 Appellate Brief)

" [M]arijuana has an extremely wide acute margin of safety for use under medical supervision and cannot cause lethal reactions ... [G]reater harm is caused by the legal consequences of its prohibition than possible risks of medicinal use."
— American Public Health Association, Resolution #9513,

"Access to Therapeutic Marijuana/Cannabis," 1995" [T]he use of marijuana may be appropriate when prescribed by a licensed physician solely for use in alleviating pain and nausea in patients who have been diagnosed as chronically ill with life threatening disease, when all other treatments have failed."
— The Medical Society of the State of New York, May 3, 2004"

[T]here is sufficient evidence for us to support any physician-patient relationship that believes the use of  marijuana will be beneficial to the patient."
— Rhode Island Medical Society, 2004

" [The] CMA continue to support the ability of physicians to discuss and make recommendations concerning the potential benefits or harm to the patient of smoked herbal cannabis consistent with state and federal law and oppose criminal prosecution of patients who possess or use smoked herbal cannabis for medical reasons upon the recommendation of a physician."
— California Medical Association, October 30, 2006

" [I]t cannot seriously be contested that there exists a small but significant class of individuals who suffer from painful chronic,

degenerative, and terminal conditions, for whom marijuana provides uniquely effective relief."
— HIV Medicine Association of the Infectious Diseases Society of America, American Medical Students Association, Lymphoma Foundation of America, Dr. Barbara Roberts, and Irvin Rosenfeld, Amicus Curiae brief filed in the U.S. Supreme Court (in the case of *Gonzales v. Raich*), October 2004

"Because inhaled smoked cannabis has more favorable pharmacokinetics than administration via oral or other routes, research should focus on the development of an inhaled mode of administration that gives results as close to smoked cannabis as possible."
— National Multiple Sclerosis Society,

"Recommendations Regarding the Use of Cannabis in Multiple Sclerosis," Expert Opinion Paper, July 2008 "There are sufficient data available to suggest that cannabinoids may have neuroprotective effects that studies in this area should be aggressively pursued."
— National Multiple Sclerosis Society, "Recommendations Regarding the Use of Cannabis in Multiple Sclerosis," Expert Opinion Paper, July 2008

" We think people who use cannabis to relieve the pain of arthritis should be able to do so."
— Arthritis Research Campaign, October 23, 2001

" Whitman-Walker Clinic supports the valid use of marijuana, under a physician's supervision, to help alleviate AIDS wasting syndrome and nausea associated with treatment regimes."
— Whitman-Walker Clinic, April 1998

" [F]or cancer patients with advanced cancers who want to improve the quality of their life, a risk versus benefit analysis [of smoked medical marijuana] weighs heavily on the benefit side."
— *Cancer Monthly*, May 2006

"[B]ased on much evidence from patients and doctors alike on the superior effectiveness and safety of whole cannabis ... we hereby petition the Executive Branch and the Congress to facilitate and expedite the research necessary to determine whether this substance should be licensed for medical use by seriously ill persons."
— Federation of American Scientists, petition to the U.S. Health and Human Services Secretary, November 1994

" In states where patients are permitted to use marijuana medicinally for serious and/or chronic illnesses and a patient's physician has recommended its use in accordance with that state's law and that state's medical practice standards, the patient should not be subject to federal criminal penalties for such medical use."
— HIV Medicine Association, October 30, 2006

" The American Medical Student Association strongly urges the United States government ... to reschedule marijuana to Schedule II of the Controlled Substance Act, and ... end the medical prohibition against marijuana."
— American Medical Students Association, March 1993

" [We] recommend that the APA support the AMA recommendation, 'The AMA believes that effective patient care requires the free and unfettered exchange of information on treatment and alternatives and that discussion of these

alternatives between physicians and patients should not subject either party to criminal sanctions.'"
— Assembly of the American Psychiatric Association, November 3, 2007 (Note: This language has not been yet been adopted as official policy of the APA)

" [We] support protection for patients and physicians participating in state approved medical marijuana programs."
— Assembly of the American Psychiatric Association, November 3, 2007 (Note: This language has not been yet been adopted as official policy of the APA)

" [The LFA] urges Congress and the President to enact legislation to reschedule marijuana to allow doctors to prescribe smokable marijuana to patients in need ... [and] urges the U.S. Public Health Service to allow limited access to medicinal marijuana by promptly reopening the Investigational New Drug compassionate access program to new applicants."
— Lymphoma Foundation of America, January 20, 1997

" [We] support the right of physicians to recommend marijuana for limited medical purposes, consistent with prevailing state laws. [We] recommend that patients be protected when in possession of and/or using legal quantities of marijuana under physician supervision in state-sanctioned medical marijuana programs. [We] recommend to the federal government that it revise its current policies that subject patients to the threat of federal arrest and prosecution even though they are under physician supervision and in possession of legal quantities of medical marijuana under state-sanctioned programs."
—Marijuana: Medical Use Action Paper endorsed by various members of the American Psychiatric Association in leadership

positions, including seven past presidents, two trustees, and the APA Lifers, November 2007

" [A] federal policy that prohibits physicians from alleviating suffering by prescribing marijuana for seriously ill patients is misguided, heavy-handed, and inhumane."
— Dr. Jerome Kassirer, "Federal Foolishness and Marijuana," editorial, *New England Journal of Medicine*, January 30, 1997"

[T]he American Association for Social Psychiatry supports full legal status for states to implement their own doctor-advised, medical marijuana programs for patients with serious physical medical conditions ... [T]he American Association for Social Psychiatry strongly urge that in a state where patients are permitted to use marijuana medicinally for serious and/or chronic illnesses and a patient's physician has recommended its use in accordance with that state's law and that state's medical practice standards, the patient should not be subject to federal criminal penalties for such medical use."
— American Association for Social Psychiatry, May 20, 2007

"Federal drug policy on marijuana threatens the health and well being of thousands of Americans by prohibiting even the medicinal use of cannabis under physician supervision in states with medical marijuana laws. The federal government has actively impeded research on the medical use of marijuana despite patient and physician reports that it may help to relieve such debilitating symptoms as nausea, pain, and loss of appetite associated with serious illnesses... [t]he SSSP supports both the Hinchey-Rohrabacher medical marijuana amendment and the Medical Marijuana Patient Protection Act."

—Society for the Study of Social Problems, "Resolution: Medical Marijuana," August 2008

"[We] support pharmacy participation in the legal distribution of medical marijuana."
— California Pharmacists Association, May 26, 1997

"Government positions on the control of drugs sometimes does not seem to reflect emerging scientific research and advice though they may meet with public and media support ... Where reputable doctors believe that a substance has a beneficial and measurable effect on the health of individual patients far outweighing any potential harmful side-effects, and where there is research or sound evidence to support such a belief, there should be a mechanism to allow such an individual to benefit from that substance while protecting the public in general."
—Amnesty International, "AI and the Medical use of Marijuana," June 2008

" The evidence is overwhelming that marijuana can relieve certain types of pain, nausea, vomiting and other symptoms caused by illnesses like multiple sclerosis, cancer and AIDS — or by the harsh drugs sometimes used to treat them. And it can do so with remarkable safety. Indeed, marijuana is less toxic than many of the drugs that physicians prescribe every day."
— former U.S. Surgeon General Joycelyn Elders, M.D., "Myths About Medical Marijuana," *Providence Journal*, March 26, 2004

"We must make sure that the casualties of the war on drugs are not suffering patients who legitimately deserve relief."
— Scott Fishman, president of the American Academy of Pain Medicine, February 2006

" It [medical marijuana] should be an option for patients who have it recommended by knowledgeable physicians."
— Dr. Jesse L. Steinfeld, former U.S. Surgeon General, July 2003

" Marijuana, in its natural form, is one of the safest therapeutically active substances known ... The evidence in this record clearly shows that marijuana has been accepted as capable of relieving the distress of great numbers of very ill people, and doing so with safety under medical supervision. It would be unreasonable, arbitrary and capricious for [the] DEA to continue to stand between those sufferers and the benefits of this substance."
— Francis L. Young, DEA Chief Administrative Law Judge, 1988

" I consider the most important recommendation made by the IOM (Institute of Medicine) panel [to be] that physicians be able to prescribe marijuana to individual patients with debilitating or terminal conditions ... I believe such compassionate use is justified."
— Andrew Weil, M.D., July 1999

" Cannabinoids and THC also have strong pain-killing powers, which is one reason medical marijuana should be readily available to people with cancer and other debilitating diseases."
— Dean Edell, M.D., March 2, 2000

" I'm an oncologist as well as an AIDS doctor, and I don't think that a drug that creates euphoria in patients with terminal diseases is having an adverse effect."
— Donald Abrams, M.D. 2005

" Cannabis will one day be seen as a wonder drug, as was penicillin in the 1940s. Like penicillin, herbal marijuana is remarkably

nontoxic, has a wide range of therapeutic applications and would be quite inexpensive if it were legal."
— Dr. Lester Grinspoon, professor of psychiatry at Harvard Medical School, *Los Angeles Times*, May 5, 2006

" Not everybody needs marijuana for medical illness. But for those who really do, it's very helpful. As more and more states are taking medical marijuana – New Mexico just did it the other day – eventually it will just be overwhelming. And it will happen. But I'm shocked that it's taken this long."
— Dr. Thomas Ungerleider, Professor Emeritus of psychiatry at UCLA and member of President Nixon's National Commission on Marijuana and Drug Abuse, "3rd Degree," *LA City Beat*, March 29, 2007

" Overall, by comparison with other drugs used mainly for 'recreational' purposes, cannabis could be rated to be a relatively safe drug ... In contrast, cannabis might have beneficial effects in some medical indications ... It seems likely that medicinal cannabis will re-enter the pharmacopeia."
— Dr. Leslie Iversen, pharmacologist at Oxford University and member of the British government's Advisory Council on the Misuse of Drugs, "Long-term effects of exposure to cannabis," *Current Opinion in Pharmacology*, 2005

" Cannabinoids, the active components of cannabis sativa and their derivatives ... exert palliative effects in patients with cancer and inhibit tumour growth in laboratory animals."
— Dr. Manuel Guzman, associate professor of biochemistry and molecular biology at Complutense University, Madrid, Spain, "Cannabinoids: Potential Anti-Cancer Agents," *Nature Reviews — Cancer*, October 2003

" 54% of oncologists favor the controlled medical availability of marijuana, and 44% have advised at least one of their cancer patients to obtain marijuana illegally. "
— Doblin/Kleiman (Harvard University) scientifically valid, random survey of oncologists, *Journal of Clinical Oncology*, 1990

" I have spent my entire career in search of more effective treatments for this awful disease [amyotrophic lateral sclerosis (ALS, aka Lou Gehrig's disease)]. We have now found that the cannabinoids, the active ingredients in medical marijuana, work remarkably well in controlling the clinical symptoms of ALS. Even more exciting is that we are now discovering that the cannabinoids actually protect nerve cells and may prolong the life of patients with ALS. "
— Gregory Carter, M.D., clinical professor of Rehabilitation Medicine, University of Washington School of Medicine, and co-director, Muscular Dystrophy Association (MDA)/Amyotrophic Lateral Sclerosis (ALS) Center (testimony submitted to Illinois Senate Public Health Committee, March 2007)

" There is no problem, basically, with marijuana as a medicine ... Marijuana is no different than morphine, no different than codeine, no different than Aspirin. "
— Health Canada's Jeremy Mercer, "'We Will Approve Marijuana Prescriptions: Marijuana 'No Different than Aspirin,' Health Canada official says," *Ottawa Citizen*, December 19, 1997

" [R]esearch has shown that cannabis can be of medicinal use. ... This is an area where public health must prevail. "
— Belgian Ministry of Health, Willem Scholten, "Statement of the Health Ministry," IACM Conference, Brussels, September 4, 2003

" Despite the positive appraisal of the therapeutic potential of cannabinoids ..., they have not been widely used ... Part of the reason for this is that research on the therapeutic use of these compounds has become a casualty of the debate in the United States about the legal status of cannabis ... As a community we do not allow this type of thinking to deny the use of opiates for analgesia. Nor should it be used to deny access to any therapeutic uses of cannabinoid derivatives that may be revealed by pharmacological research."
— Australian National Task Force on Cannabis, Wayne Hall, Nadia Solowij, and Jim Lemon, "The health and psychological consequences of cannabis use," *National Drug Strategy Monograph Series No. 25*, 1994,

" People can debate marijuana's potential for abuse, but it is increasingly clear that cannabis has definite medicinal benefits. Studies and abundant anecdotal evidence demonstrate that marijuana can stimulate the appetites of people with AIDS and cancer, reduce nausea in chemotherapy patients, and help people with such debilitating conditions as multiple sclerosis, diabetes and glaucoma."
— Wesley J. Smith, senior fellow at the Discovery Institute, *San Francisco Chronicle*, December 2, 2007

" So let's get this straight: I am against the legalization of marijuana ... However, there are cases when marijuana makes sense, like in medicine. There are a host of serious diseases when smoking pot is the best and sometimes the only relief for pain and suffering. There are plenty of people who abuse all sorts of prescription drugs, but law-abiding citizens can still have access if they need them. So, when I read about the Drug Enforcement Agency, the DEA, raiding ten medical marijuana clinics in California last week,

totally legal businesses. I have to agree with the critics that call this case, and the DEA, bullies."
— Glenn Beck, August 3, 2007

" The National Nurses Society on Addictions urges the federal government to remove marijuana from the Schedule I category immediately, and make it available for physicians to prescribe. NNSA urges the American Nurses Association and other health care professional organizations to support patient access to this medicine."
— National Nurses Society on Addictions, May 1, 1995

" Marijuana has proven to be effective in the treatment of people with HIV/AIDS, multiple sclerosis, cancer, and those suffering from severe pain or nausea ... The legalization of medical marijuana would be a step forward for the health of all New Yorkers."
— New York State Association of County Health Officials, resolution, 2003

" The SFMS takes a support[ive] position on the California Medical Marijuana Initiative [legalizing medical marijuana]."
— San Francisco Medical Society, August 1996

" [The American Bar Association] recognizes that persons who suffer from serious illnesses for which marijuana has a medically recognized therapeutic value have a right to be treated with marijuana under the supervision of a physician."
— American Bar Association, May 4, 1998

" If Cannabis were unknown, and bio-prospectors were suddenly to find it in some remote mountain crevice, its discovery would no doubt be hailed as a medical breakthrough. Scientists would praise its potential for treating everything from pain to cancer, and marvel at its rich pharmacopoeia — many of whose chemicals mimic vital molecules in the human body."

— "Reefer Madness, Marijuana Is Medically Useful Whether Politicians Like It or Not," *The Economist*, April 29, 2006

## Also available from author, Michael Malott

**The Michigan Medical Marijuana Handbook** is an essential must have for every Michigan medical marijuana patient, caregiver and dispensary. This handy reference guide touches base on all important topics about medical marijuana, its use in the treatment of illnesses and disease, scientific facts, an independent section on marijuana laws. A section on how to handle interaction with law enforcement, important legal facts about the Patriot Act, Plain View Doctrine, probable cause, reasonable suspicion, and warrantless searches.

The guide also looks at state and federal law regarding marijuana and medical marijuana, possession, use and cultivation. Other topics include a complete section on applying for a Michigan medical marijuana ID card, facts on marijuana contaminates and sterilizing medical marijuana. A section featuring over 500 strains of cannabis and each strains recommended medical use and effect.

Michael Malott

ISBN: 978-1461068099

ISBN: 978-1463514037

**The Arizona Medical Marijuana Handbook** is a huge 300+ page essential must have for every Arizona medical marijuana patient, caregiver and dispensary. This handy reference guide touches base on all important topics about medical marijuana, its use in the treatment of illnesses and disease, scientific facts, an independent section on marijuana laws. A section on how to handle interaction with law enforcement, important legal facts about the Patriot Act, Plain View Doctrine, probable cause, reasonable suspicion, and warrantless searches.

The guide also looks at state and federal law regarding marijuana and medical marijuana, possession, use and cultivation. Other topics include a complete section on applying for a Arizona medical marijuana ID card, facts on marijuana contaminates and sterilizing medical marijuana. A section featuring over 500 strains of cannabis and each strains recommended medical use and effect. This guide includes the entire text of the Arizona Medical Marijuana Laws and more.

The Arizona Medical Marijuana Handbook is packed full of useful information and facts covering the highly controversial medical marijuana issue.

223

ISBN: 978-1466343382

Medical Marijuana Laws is a legal reference guide featuring the actual text of the medical marijuana laws of all current states which have adopted medical marijuana laws despite federal laws prohibiting such. Each states laws are presented in their actual and concise form as written when passed in each respective state.

An outstanding legal reference for anyone interested in researching each state's laws and construction of their regulations.

The Medical Marijuana Patient's Guide is a handy reference guide which touches base on all important topics about medical marijuana, its use in the treatment of illness and disease, scientific facts and a comprehensive section on law. The guide also takes a look at federal law regarding marijuana and medical marijuana, possession, use and cultivation. Each states medical marijuana laws are also examined.

ISBN: 978-1466316454

224

ALSO CURRENTLY AVAILABLE FROM
AUTHOR AND ACTIVIST
## MICHAEL MALOTT

## MEDICAL MARIJUANA
The Story of Dennis Peron, the San Francisco Cannabis Buyers Club and the Ensuing Road to Decriminalization

Dennis Peron is the person behind the legalization of medical marijuana in the State of California. In the mid 90's, Dennis opened the legendary S.F. Cannabis Buyers Club. A five-story storefront, which openly distributed hundreds of pounds of medical marijuana daily to sick and dying patients. Despite its main street location, the club continued to openly sell marijuana without interference by police or city officials under the protection of CA. Prop. 215, which allowed the use of medical marijuana with a doctor's recommendation. Eventually State Attorney General, Dan Lundgren and his officers raided the club. The raid opened the door to one of the most publicized and criticized police acts in the history of the legal system. Lundgren felt repercussions through the San Francisco Police Department, city hall, the mayor's office all the way to Washington, D.C. Lundgren was shunned for using the raid as a platform for himself for the upcoming Democratic Convention which had been only days away. Everyone all the way up to local churches stepped up and started to distribute medical marijuana to San Francisco's sick and dying. Thousands gathered to protest Lungren's actions and Dennis and the San Francisco Cannabis Buyers Club was thrust into the worldwide media spotlight in one of the most controversial legal issues of this century. Lungren was criticized all the way to Washington D.C. and Peron became a real American hero. At present day, literally hundreds of cannabis buyers clubs now openly distribute medical marijuana throughout California. Medical recommendations are freely distributed to thousands of California residents for anything from anxiety to AIDS. Oakland is now commonly referred to as "Oaksterdam" and reminiscent of Amsterdam, clubs fill the downtown area right next store to city hall. This is the story of one incredible man who had compassion, vision, and a dream, and against impossible odds he made it a reality.

**Available at Amazon or through major book stores everywhere**

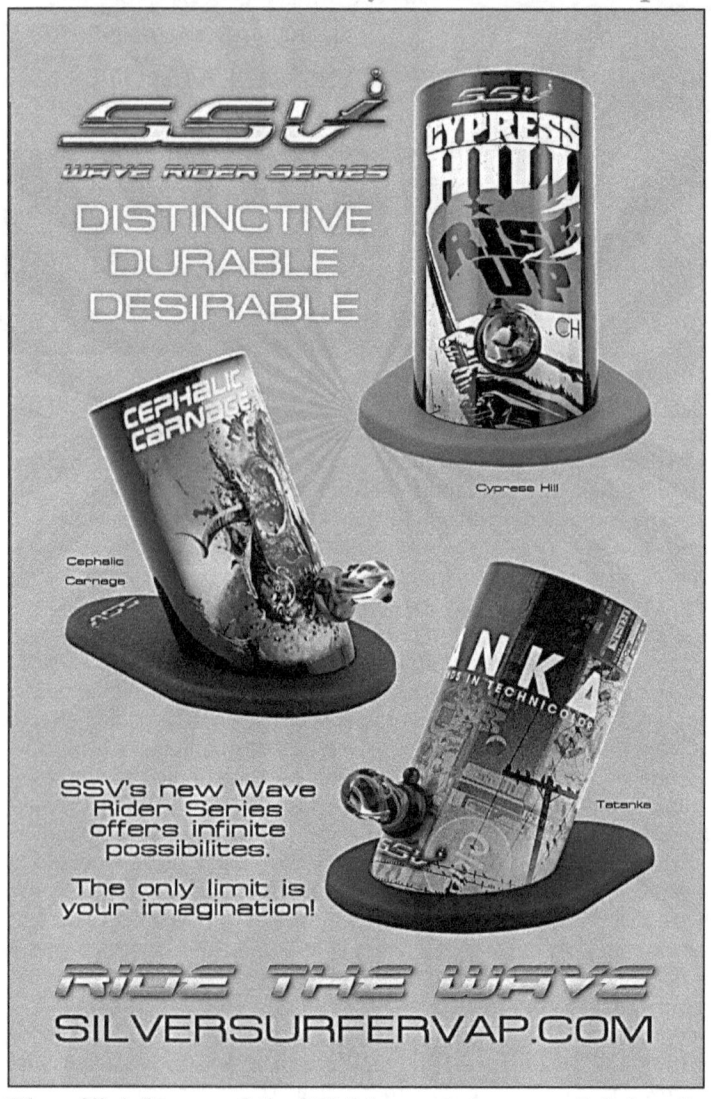

## PERSONAL STRAIN NOTES

_____

_____

_____

_____

_____

_____

_____

_____

_____

_____

_____

_____

_____

_____

_____

_____

_____

_____

_____

_____

_____

_____

_____

_____

_____

# PERSONAL STRAIN NOTES

# PERSONAL STRAIN NOTES

# PERSONAL STRAIN NOTES

# PERSONAL STRAIN NOTES

www.ingramcontent.com/pod-product-compliance
Lightning Source LLC
Chambersburg PA
CBHW070416290526
45791CB00005B/1725